NEW ZEALAND
DRIVING HOLIDAYS

Lake Wanaka – Deerace Publishing

CONTENTS

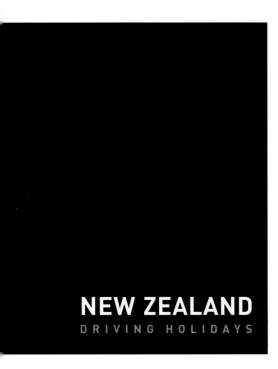

NEW ZEALAND
DRIVING HOLIDAYS

INTRODUCTION

New Zealand is the perfect destination to tour by car. Its roads are well formed and un-cluttered, its tourist infrastructure world class, and New Zealanders take seriously their commitment to protecting, as well as making accessible, the beauty of their natural environment. As committed globetrotters themselves, kiwis combine pride in their homeland with empathy for fellow travellers and this is reflected in the warm welcome visitors often comment upon, even found in far-flung corners of the country. However, like their feathery namesakes, kiwis are known to shun the limelight and many a world-class experience is tucked away behind an unassuming exterior far off the beaten track. A self-drive tour allows you the freedom to create your own unique and memorable holiday, and local knowledge is the key that unlocks a world of hidden delights.

This book is the result of a happy collaboration between a New Zealand travel writer/photographer, an overseas family friend, and Apex Car Rentals, New Zealand's largest independently owned car hire company. A few months ago, two emails landed in my inbox at the same time. One was a commission from Apex Car Rentals to write this book, and the other was from Bob, befriended by my family on one of their globetrotting expeditions. He knew I was a travel writer specialising in driving excursions and holidays in New Zealand, and as he was planning a trip, he decided to look me up for some advice on where to go and what to see. As a great believer in serendipity I took a leap and invited Bob to join me on what we later dubbed "The Great New Zealand Road (and Food) (and Wine) (and Fishing) Trip".

We enjoyed a leisurely journey with Apex Car Rentals exploring the country from Cape Reinga to Bluff. We took our time to enjoy the highlights and kept a record of our experiences. To this end, we spent an utterly wonderful eight weeks sampling regional food and wine; meeting local characters; marvelling at the distinctive natural environment of this unique corner of the planet; perusing museums, galleries and craft boutiques; subjecting ourselves to various crazy adventures; and absorbing local culture. Having spent three decades exploring every corner of these unique islands I call home, it was an absolute delight for me to take on the role of guide, and to share my passion for New Zealand with a first-timer as enthusiastic as Bob. He was enchanted with everything, fell in love with the ever-changing panorama of delights that unfolded before us, and his spirits (and appetite) never flagged.

The end result, is a true "insider's guide" to New Zealand. The itineraries enable visitors to see the country at a pace that leaves time to savour the moment, with breakout options highlighting day trips of special interest. You could also select from different itineraries to create your own pathway through this fascinating land. Whether you choose the beaten track or the road less travelled, I am sure you will come to agree, that these islands that some four million people call home, are a very special place indeed.

TOURING
NEW ZEALAND

Moeraki Boulders - Deerace Publishing

New Zealand is an archipelago comprising some 700 islands and offers many dramatically contrasting scenic routes for the intrepid traveller to explore. The majority of touring routes are found on the North and South Islands. Stewart Island, New Zealand's third largest isle, has a land mass of approximately 1746 kilometres square but remains relatively isolated with few roads and only some 200 permanent residents, most of whom live in the small town of Oban.

The North Island

Adventure beckons throughout New Zealand's North Island, and unique scenery awaits. In subtropical Northland proud forests of majestic kauri trees, some thousands of years old, share space with remnants of its gumdigging past. Gnarled pohutukawa cling to windswept cliffs over golden beaches, and green rolling hills of farmland span across the island from coast to coast. Although the North Island's land mass is smaller than that of the South Island, it boasts a longer coastline with hundreds of deep tranquil harbours, estuaries and inlets with sheltered, sandy bays providing safe anchorage for boats.

Thermal activity abounds: there's Rotorua, a hotbed of fiery fury with its boiling mud pools, geysers, springs and spas; White Island, an active volcano in the Bay of Plenty; and volcanic Auckland whose 50 or so 'hills' are also the result of volcanic activity. Hot springs are dotted throughout the North Island and one of the country's most unique experiences is to dig your own warm spa in the sand at Te Puia Springs in Kawhia, or at the Coromanel's aptly named Hot Water Beach.

At the heart of the North Island lie the crystal-clear waters of Lake Taupo, New Zealand's largest lake, itself a huge volcanic crater fed by the mountains of the Central Plateau. These formidable mountains - Tongariro, Ngauruhoe and Ruapehu - are encircled by dry, desert like plains that contrast dramatically with the surrounding fertile farmlands. To the west a bulbous coastline horseshoes around Mt Taranaki, while to the east lies the seldom-explored East Cape. Hidden beneath hills beside the Wellington Harbour, also formed by volcanic eruption and now filled with sea, the capital city of Wellington is the departure point to the magnificent South Island.

The South Island

The South Island, an awe-inspiring panorama of majestic snowy mountains, dripping rainforest, silent fiords and sounds, ancient glaciers, wide open plains, and blue lakes and rivers, is home to only one quarter of NZ's population. It's a place of grandeur and solitude, where visitors can truly become at one with nature. In parts you can drive for hours before meeting another soul.

At its northern tip, the regions of Marlborough and Tasman enjoy New Zealand's highest sunshine hours, while the Marlborough Sounds, a series of beautiful drowned sea valleys, is a boaties' paradise of numerous inlets, islands, peninsulas, and deep sandy coves, many of which cannot be reached by road.

The West Coast offers a wealth of contrasting scenery: in the north clusters of nikau palms sprout from glistening white sands, while to the south dense forests of beech cascade down to meet the sea. The rugged coastline features unique rock formations, deep fiords, and dense rainforests, as well as the icy tongues of Franz Josef and Fox Glaciers poking from the snowcapped Southern Alps.

These mountains, a spine of jagged mountains running the length of the South Island, were formed by a collision of tectonic plates, which, in a bid to outdo each other, force the mountains heavenwards by some 10mm per year. As it is, the Southern Alps rise to heights of over 3000 metres in places, with Aoraki (Mt Cook), New Zealand's highest mountain, dominating the range at 3,754 metres.

The small picturesque towns of Wanaka, Te Anau and Queenstown nestle amongst the alps beside shimmering lakes and provide a base for adventure and outdoor activities including hiking, skiing, whitewater rafting, jetboating and bungy jumping – just to name a few.

To the east genteel towns bask amid farming plains beneath the Southern Alps and provide a home to most of the South Island's inhabitants. The largest of these is the city of Christchurch, well known for its beautiful gardens set beside the clear waters of the Avon River, and an excellent starting point for any scenic tour of New Zealand.

NORTH ISLAND ITINERARIES

Auckland to Auckland

FOUR DAY NORTHLAND DRIVE
Day one – Auckland to Paihia
Day two – Paihia to Cape Reinga
Day three – Cape Reinga to Opononi
Day four – Opononi to Auckland

FOUR DAY THERMAL DRIVE
Day one – Auckland to Whitianga
Day two – Whitianga to Whakatane
Day three – Whakatane to Rotorua
Day four – Rotorua to Auckland

FOUR DAY CENTRAL LOOP DRIVE
Day one – Auckland to Rotorua
Day two – Rotorua to Taupo
Day three – Taupo to Waitomo
Day four – Waitomo to Auckland

SEVEN DAY FIGURE OF EIGHT DRIVE
Day one – Auckland to Paihia
Day two – Paihia to Cape Reinga
Day three – Cape Reinga to Opononi
Day four – Opononi to Muriwai Beach
Day five – Muriwai Beach to Whitianga
Day six – Whitianga to Waitomo
Day seven – Waitomo to Auckland

SEVEN DAY EAST COAST DRIVE
Day one – Auckland to Whitianga
Day two – Whitianga to Whakatane
Day three – Whakatane to Gisborne
Day four – Gisborne to Napier
Day five – Napier to Taupo
Day six – Taupo to Rotorua
Day seven – Rotorua to Auckland

SEVEN DAY WEST COAST DRIVE
Day one – Auckland to Whitianga
Day two – Whitianga to Rotorua

Day three – Rotorua to Taupo
Day four – Taupo to Wanganui
Day five – Wanganui to Hawera
Day six – Hawera to Waitomo
Day seven – Waitomo to Auckland

FOURTEEN DAY NORTH ISLAND HIGHLIGHTS
Day one – Auckland to Paihia
Day two – Paihia to Cape Reinga
Day three – Cape Reinga to Opononi
Day four – Opononi to Muriwai Beach
Day five – Muriwai Beach to Whitianga
Day six – Whitianga to Whakatane
Day seven – Whakatane to Gisborne
Day eight – Gisborne to Napier
Day nine – Napier to Taupo
Day ten – Taupo to Wanganui
Day eleven – Wanganui to New Plymouth
Day twelve – New Plymouth to Waitomo
Day thirteen – Waitomo to Rotorua
Day fourteen – Rotorua to Auckland

Auckland to Wellington

FOUR DAY EAST COAST DRIVE
Day one – Auckland to Whakatane
Day two – Whakatane to Gisborne
Day three – Gisborne to Napier
Day four – Napier to Wellington

FOUR DAY WEST COAST DRIVE
Day one – Auckland to Waitomo
Day two – Waitomo to New Plymouth
Day three – New Plymouth to Wanganui
Day four – Wanganui to Wellington

SEVEN DAY CENTRAL DRIVE
Day one – Auckland to Whitianga
Day two – Whitianga to Whakatane
Day three – Whakatane to Rotorua
Day four – Rotorua to Taupo
Day five – Taupo to Ohakune

Day six – Ohakune to Palmerston North
Day seven – Palmerston North to Wellington

SEVEN DAY EAST COAST DRIVE
Day one – Auckland to Whitianga
Day two – Whitianga to Rotorua
Day three – Rotorua to Whakatane
Day four – Whakatane to Gisborne
Day five – Gisborne to Napier
Day six – Napier to Martinborough
Day seven – Martinborough to Wellington

SEVEN DAY WEST COAST DRIVE
Day one – Auckland to Waitomo
Day two – Waitomo to Rotorua
Day three – Rotorua to Taupo
Day four – Taupo to New Plymouth
Day five – New Plymouth to Wanganui
Day six – Wanganui to Wellington

FOURTEEN DAY NORTH ISLAND HIGHLIGHTS
Day one – Auckland to Paihia
Day two – Paihia to Cape Reinga
Day three – Cape Reinga to Opononi
Day four – Opononi to Muriwai Beach
Day five – Muriwai Beach to Whitianga
Day six – Whitianga to Whakatane
Day seven – Whakatane to Gisborne
Day eight – Gisborne to Napier
Day nine – Napier to Taupo
Day ten – Taupo to Waitomo
Day eleven – Waitomo to New Plymouth
Day twelve – New Plymouth to Wanganui
Day thirteen – Wanganui to Palmerston Nth
Day fourteen – Palmerston Nth to Wellington

Wellington to Wellington

FOUR DAY SOUTHERN DRIVE
Day one – Wellington to Wanganui
Day two – Wanganui to Napier
Day three – Napier to Martinborough
Day four – Martinborough to Wellington

Nugget Point - Venture Southland Tourism

SOUTH ISLAND ITINERARIES

Christchurch to Christchurch

FOUR DAY SPRINGS DRIVE
Day one – Christchurch to Kaikoura
Day two – Kaikoura to Blenheim
Day three – Blenheim to Hanmer Springs
Day four – Hanmer Springs to Christchurch

FOUR DAY WESTERN LOOP DRIVE
Day one – Christchurch to Hanmer Springs
Day two – Hanmer Springs to Westport
Day three – Westport to Greymouth
Day four – Greymouth to Christchurch

FOUR DAY MT COOK DRIVE
Day one – Christchurch to Timaru
Day two – Timaru to Oamaru
Day three – Oamaru to Mt Cook
Day four – Mt Cook to Christchurch

SEVEN DAY NORTHERN DRIVE
Day one – Christchurch to Kaikoura
Day two – Kaikoura to Blenheim
Day three – Blenheim to Nelson
Day four – Nelson to Collingwood
Day five – Collingwood to Murchison
Day six – Murchison to Greymouth
Day seven – Greymouth to Christchurch

SEVEN DAY WESTERN DRIVE
Day one – Christchurch to Hanmer Springs
Day two – Hanmer Springs to Greymouth
Day three – Greymouth to Franz Josef
Day four – Franz Josef to Wanaka
Day five – Wanaka to Queenstown
Day six – Queenstown to Mt Cook
Day seven – Mt Cook to Christchurch

SEVEN DAY SOUTHERN DRIVE
Day one – Christchurch to Timaru
Day two – Timaru to Oamaru

Day three – Oamaru to Dunedin
Day four – Dunedin to Alexandra
Day five – Alexandra to Queenstown
Day six – Queenstown to Mt Cook
Day seven – Mt Cook to Christchurch

FOURTEEN DAY SOUTH ISLAND HIGHLIGHTS
Day one – Christchurch to Kaikoura
Day two – Kaikoura to Blenheim
Day three – Blenheim to Nelson
Day four – Nelson to Murchison
Day five – Murchison to Greymouth
Day six – Greymouth to Franz Josef
Day seven – Franz Josef to Wanaka
Day eight – Wanaka to Alexandra
Day nine – Alexandra to Queenstown
Day ten – Queenstown to Te Anau
Day eleven – Te Anau to Riverton
Day twelve – Riverton to Dunedin
Day thirteen – Dunedin to Oamaru
Day fourteen – Oamaru to Christchurch

Christchurch to Picton

FOUR DAY SPRINGS DRIVE
Day one – Christchurch to Hanmer Springs
Day two – Hanmer Springs to Kaikoura
Day three – Kaikoura to Blenheim
Day four – Blenheim to Picton

FOUR DAY WESTERN DRIVE
Day one – Christchurch to Greymouth
Day two – Greymouth to Westport
Day three – Westport to Nelson
Day four – Nelson to Picton

SEVEN DAY WESTERN DRIVE
Day one – Christchurch to Kaikoura
Day two – Kaikoura to Hanmer Springs
Day three – Hanmer Springs to Greymouth
Day four – Greymouth to Westport
Day five – Westport to Murchison

Day six – Murchison to Nelson
Day seven – Nelson to Picton

SEVEN DAY NORTHERN DRIVE
Day one – Christchurch to Greymouth
Day two – Greymouth to Westport
Day three – Westport to Murchison
Day four – Murchison to Hanmer Springs
Day five – Hanmer Springs to Kaikoura
Day six – Kaikoura to Blenheim
Day seven – Blenheim to Picton

SEVEN DAY SOUTHERN DRIVE
Day one – Christchurch to Timaru
Day two – Timaru to Mt Cook
Day three – Mt Cook to Wanaka
Day four – Wanaka to Franz Josef
Day five – Franz Josef to Greymouth
Day six – Greymouth to Murchison
Day seven – Murchison to Picton

FOURTEEN DAY SOUTH ISLAND HIGHLIGHTS
Day one – Christchurch to Oamaru
Day two – Oamaru to Mt Cook
Day three – Mt Cook to Alexandra
Day four – Alexandra to Dunedin
Day five – Dunedin to Riverton
Day six – Riverton to Te Anau
Day seven – Te Anau to Queenstown
Day eight – Queenstown to Wanaka
Day nine – Wanaka to Franz Josef
Day ten – Franz Josef to Greymouth
Day eleven – Greymouth to Murchison
Day twelve – Murchison to Kaikoura
Day thirteen – Kaikoura to Nelson
Day fourteen – Nelson to Picton

Picton to Picton

FOUR DAY NORTHERN DRIVE
Day one – Picton to Nelson
Day two – Nelson to Murchison
Day three – Murchison to Golden Bay
Day four – Golden Bay to Picton

Golden Bay
Collingwood
Takaka
ABEL TASMAN NATIONAL PARK
60
Tasman Bay
KAHURANGI NATIONAL PARK
Motueka
Karamea
Karamea Bight
Brightwater
Richmond
Havelock
Nelson
Picton
Wakefield
Renwick
Blenheim
Seddon
L. Grassmere
Westport
67
Murchison
Ward
6
PAPAROA NATIONAL PARK
69
Reefton
65
NELSON LAKES NATIONAL PARK
1
Punakaiki
7
Hanmer Springs
Kaikoura
Greymouth
Lake Brunner
7
7A
Kumara
70
Culverden
Waiau
Hokitika
Cheviot
ARTHURS PASS NATIONAL PARK
Hawarden
Ross
Arthur's Pass
73
Waikari
Waipara
TASMAN SEA
Amberley
Pegasus Bay
Harihari
Oxford
Sefton
Leithfield
Springfield
Rangiora
Woodend
Cust
Whataroa
Sheffield
Kaiapoi
Franz Josef Glacier
WESTLAND NATIONAL PARK
Darfield
Kirwee
Christchurch
Fox Glacier
Mount Hutt
Hororata
Rolleston
Lyttelton
Methven
Dunsandel
Lincoln
MOUNT COOK NATIONAL PARK
Rakaia
Leeston
75
Mount Cook
77
Southbridge
Akaroa
Lake Tekapo
Ashburton
Haast
1
Geraldine
79
Jackson Bay
Fairlie
Pleasant Point
Canterbury Bight
8
Temuka
Lake Pukaki
8
Timaru
Twizel
MOUNT ASPIRING NATIONAL PARK
6
Otematata
Big Bay
Lake Ohau
83
Waimate
Lake Aviemore
82
Kurow
Milford Sound
Milford Sound
PACIFIC OCEAN
Wanaka
Naseby
8A
Oamaru
Arrowtown
Kakanui
65
Herbert
Queenstown
Cromwell
Ranfurly
Hampden
FIORDLAND NATIONAL PARK
Clyde
Doubtful Sound
Alexandra
Middlemarch
Palmerston
94
87
Waikouaiti
Karitane
Te Anau
Roxburgh
Warrington
Port Chalmers
95
6
Waitati
Mosgiel
Manapouri
8
Dunedin
Lake Manapouri
Lumsden
Heriot
Outram
Mossburn
Kelso
Lawrence
Ohai
Riversdale
Tapanui
1
Brighton
Nightcaps
94
90
Lake Monowai
L. Hauroko
Gore
Milton
Tuatapere
Winton
Clinton
99
Otautau
Mataura
Balclutha
Makarewa
Wyndham
Kaitangata
Wallacetown
95
Edendale
Riverton
1
Owaka
Invercargill
Te Waewae Bay
Tokanui
Foveaux Strait
Bluff
Mason Bay
Halfmoon Bay
Paterson Inlet
Port Adventure
Port Pegasus

NEW ZEALAND

DRIVING HOLIDAYS

ACCOMMODATION ADVICE

Choosing accommodation in New Zealand can present a conundrum especially when you are not familiar with the terms used to describe what is available. To assist we have provided a brief outline below.

If you are holidaying in New Zealand during the height of summer, from December through to February, we strongly recommend that you pre-book your accommodation at least two weeks in advance.

Campgrounds and Holiday Parks

Campgrounds and holiday parks provide facilities for campers and those travelling in motorhomes. All properties provide communal kitchens, toilets, showers and laundry facilities. The majority provide additional features which may include a TV room, games room, a children's playground and dump stations. Most are in scenic and convenient locations and some also offer cabins and tourist flats.

Cabins

This basic, but affordable accommodation is available at many campgrounds and holiday parks. In their simplest form they consist of a bed in a room and guests are required to make use of the campground's communal facilities. You may use your own sleeping bags or hire linen if required.

Tourist Flats

Tourist Flats are also usually located in campgrounds and holiday parks. They provide a step up from cabins and come with their own bathroom and toilet facilities. Linen is also provided.

Backpackers and Hostels

Backpacker accommodation provides a mixture of shared accommodation from dormitory rooms through to double and twin rooms. Most backpackers and hostels also have a limited number of single rooms. Some provide linen, or it is available for hire. The bathroom, toilet, living room, dining room and kitchen facilities are shared.

Motel and Apartments

Motels are also commonly known as motor lodges or motor inns and suit both independent and group travellers. The majority offer fully equipped self-catering facilities with kitchens and bathrooms and are conveniently located for those travelling by car. Parking is usually provided right outside your door. Some motel units are able to accommodate up to six people, although most cater for two adults or a family of four. Accommodation options at the top end of this category are frequently referred to as Apartments.

Hotels

Hotels range from larger central city hotels which provide full conference and recreation facilities to smaller family owned and operated boutique hotels. Most offer at least one licensed bar and restaurant with facilities to charge-back to your room. Breakfast is eaten in the restaurant, or ordered through room service.

Bed and Breakfast (B&B)

B&Bs offer homely accommodation with lots of personal care and attention. It's the perfect choice for those who wish to discover more about the kiwi lifestyle. Rooms are usually provided in your host's own home and come with an en suite or private bathroom facilities. Some have their own separate entrance so you may come and go as you please.

Self Contained Bed and Breakfast

This type of accommodation offers greater flexibility and freedom yet allows guests to mingle with hosts, or not, as they wish. All come with their own private bathroom or en suite and most offer a fully equipped kitchenette.

Self Contained Cottages

This type of accommodation can be found at B&Bs or on private properties or farms. Most offer fully equipped self-catering facilities with kitchens and bathrooms. Breakfast is usually provided on request.

Farmstays and Homestays

This type of accommodation provides a unique opportunity to experience a slice of life in New Zealand's rural towns and on isolated high country stations. Although guests have their own rooms, usually with an en suite or private bathroom, they share home cooked meals with their hosts and have the opportunity to take part in sheep shearing, lambing, milking cows, working dogs and moving stock, or harvesting produce – whatever is happening on the farm at the time.

Boutique Accommodation

Boutique accommodations are those which provide several unique features or have a special ambience and warmth. They may be housed in a historical building, offer outstanding views, or be superior and memorable in other ways. Boutique accommodation can include B&Bs, self contained B&Bs, lodges and self contained cottages.

Lodges

Lodges tend to provide accommodation at the highest end of the market and are exclusive establishments with the finest facilities, locations, activities and standard of service to be found in New Zealand. Rooms of the highest standard come with en suite bathrooms. Dinner, which is usually included in the tariff, is served with other guests.

HIRING A CAR

A Message From Our Sponsor

Hiring a car in New Zealand provides the freedom and flexibility to travel where you want, when you want, and to discover all the interesting and out of the way places off the beaten tourist track - the New Zealand that I write about in this book - the New Zealand that some travellers never get to see.

When it comes to choosing a car to hire in New Zealand most multinational vehicle rental companies are represented, however Apex Car Rentals, a friendly but substantial 100 % NZ owned and operated company, is undoubtedly New Zealand's preferred local provider.

Apex staff have an in-depth knowledge of New Zealand and are committed to providing outstanding customer service every step of the way. From the moment you arrive in NZ or step into any of Apex's eleven conveniently located branches, the Apex team is on hand to ensure that the transition into a rental car is streamlined and hassle-free.

The Apex fleet includes a full line-up of new and late model sedans, hatchbacks, four wheel drive wagons, and multi-purpose vehicles. Apex also offers a range of older (three- to seven-year-old) vehicles, ideal for those travellers on a budget. All vehicles provide exceptional value for money and come with a wide range of complimentary accessories, maps and benefits.

With Apex there are no hidden costs and quoted rates include GST (NZ goods and services tax) and unlimited kilometre rates. For those travelling with children, child and booster seats are complimentary, while those travelling during the winter months are offered ski/snow board racks and snow chains for no additional charge.

Apex rates also include 24-hour Automobile Association roadside assistance cover for your peace of mind, full insurance (with a low insurance excess of $750 that may be reduced to $0 for an additional $8 per day), and one-way hires at no additional charge. Apex has branches in both Wellington and Picton and offers a complimentary vehicle exchange service to avoid the cost of transporting its rental cars across the Cook Strait.

Furthermore when you hire a car from Apex Car Rentals, there are no extra fees associated with additional drivers, senior drivers, and no pre-payments, deposits or bonds. Nor will you find booking fees, airport fees, recovery fees or pickup and drop-off fees in the fine print; in fact Apex pick-up and drop-offs are complimentary, and this includes

a transfer service to your accommodation, the railway or bus station, or airport – whatever suits your requirements!

To hire an Apex rental car you must be over 21 years of age and hold an overseas drivers license that is written in English, or hold an international drivers license.

Economy Class

Apex Economy Class is an ideal choice for up to four budget-conscious people travelling together when luggage space is not a prime consideration. Economy class features a fleet of four-door sedans (1500cc Toyota Corollas or similar). They are equipped with automatic or manual transmission, air conditioning, power steering and stereo/radio cassette and cost $NZ49 per day.

Touring Car Class

Apex Touring Car Class is ideal for a family or up to five people holidaying on a budget. Touring class features a fleet of four door sedans with larger luggage and cabin space (1800-2000cc Nissan Bluebirds or similar). They are equipped with automatic transmission, air conditioning, power steering, airbags, and stereo/radio cassette and cost $NZ59 per day.

Super Sedan Class

Apex Super Sedan Class features a fleet of new and late model 1800cc Toyota Corolla sedans with automatic transmission, air conditioning, power steering, airbags, and stereo/radio CD player. This is Apex's most popular class and is an ideal choice for couples or medium-sized family groups requiring extra comfort and space. Super Sedan Class vehicles cost $NZ69 per day.

Super Touring Class

Apex Super Touring Class features a fleet of new and late model 2400cc Toyota Camry sedans with automatic transmission, air conditioning, power steering, airbags, and stereo/radio CD player. It is the premium choice for groups of up to five people travelling together that require a vehicle with generous luggage space and good engine capacity. Super Touring Class vehicles cost $NZ79 per day.

4WD Super Wagon Class

Apex 4WD Super Wagon Class features a fleet of new and late model 2000cc four wheel drive Subaru Legacy wagon with automatic transmission, air conditioning, power steering, twin airbags, and stereo/radio CD player. It is the premium choice for medium to large groups or travellers

who intend to ski, fish, camp, or play golf and therefore need plenty of luggage room and possibly roof racks. 4WD Super Wagon class vehicles cost $NZ89 per day.

MPV Class

Larger family groups, or smaller groups requiring plenty of luggage capacity will enjoy Apex MPV Class. This fleet features eight-seater 2400cc Toyota Previa MPVs (multi purpose vehicles) with automatic transmission, dual control air conditioning, power steering, twin airbags, and stereo/radio cassette. MPV Class vehicles cost $NZ109 per day.

Freephone Contact Details

With the widespread availability of international toll-free dialing and the internet it is now feasible to arrange your rental car requirements directly with Apex before you leave home. To contact Apex Central Reservations simply dial any of the freecall numbers listed below. Alternatively, if you prefer to use the internet you will find Apex Car Rentals at www.apexrentals.com. All bookings made online are confirmed on an Instant Confirmation basis and additional discounts are offered for off-peak and extended duration hires.

From within NZ dial   0800 93 95 97
From Australia dial   0011-800-7001-8001
From USA/Canada dial 011-800-7001-8001
From UK/Ireland dial   00-800-7001-8001
From elsewhere dial   +64 3 379 6897

Rich in history and culture, Northland's sub-tropical coastline features kilometres of golden beaches, giant sand dunes, tranquil harbours, a myriad of islands and large tracts of ancient kauri forest to explore. The birthplace of the nation, it was the landing place of the great Maori adventurer Kupe, the seat of NZ's first government, and where NZ's founding document, the Treaty of Waitangi, was signed in 1840.

The three-day journey, with the optional one-day excursion to Cape Reinga, begins in Auckland. We travel the Twin Coast Highway to Paihia, take part in a traditional Maori ceremony, savour Kerikeri's gastronomic delights, take a cruise through the Bay of Islands, explore historical Russell, collect mussels from rocks in Mitimiti, and walk amongst giant kauri trees in the Waipoua Forest.

AUCKLAND TO BAY OF ISLANDS RETURN

DAY ONE
Auckland to Paihia

Following the Twin Coast Highway, we head north. It's a route I know well, but as this is the first of many journeys, I'm hoping that my travelling companion, Bob, will shape up to become a worthy co-pilot. As we leave Auckland's sprawl at Orewa, uncertainty sets in. "What's with Pie-hire?" he says jabbing his finger hopefully at Paihia, on what (in less than an hour) has fast become a crumpled page. I laugh outright; skilled navigator or otherwise, at least – if nothing else – he's a man after my own heart when it comes to food!

And so we stop in Warkworth, where life is as mellow as the river upon which it was built. On a sunny terrace we breakfast upon eggs with vivid-yellow yolks. "Do you think they add dye?" asks Bob, sipping on his latte.

We leave town driving on through Wellsford and Kaiwaka where the concrete turrets of café Utopia signal that we've entered quirkier climes. At the top of the Brynderwyns, Northland's scenery begins to unfold with the fabulous panorama of Bream Bay from the jagged silhouette of Whangarei Heads to the dramatic peaks of the Hen and Chicken Islands. Bob's still agog as we glide past Waipu and on to Ruakaka's broad sweep of sand, dominated by Marsden Point Oil Refinery's chimneystack.

A quick stretch of the legs - Bob deposits shells and a mottled crab's claw into the glovebox - and we drive to Longview Vineyard, where eighty-five-year old Milly Vuletich presses a tasting glass into our hands. The Vuletich family set up a self-sufficient winery in 1964, and Milly's son, Mario, crafts its estate-grown wines and ports.

At Whangarei's Town Basin, situated on a dock overlooking the marina, seafood chowder, full of fish and cream, is the order of the day. Later we wander past the NZ Fudge Farm's gooey treats, a host of galleries and artists' studios and stop outside Burning Issues to watch glass being blown.

Next we call into the spectacular Whangarei Falls, which plunge some 25 metres into a tranquil, bush-fringed pool. It's a leisurely 20-minute hike around the falls before we rejoin SH1 and drive to Kawakawa, where we stop to bask in the sun outside the Trainspotting Café. There are no trains to speak of (even though the tracks run the entire length of the main street) and so we watch passers-by, who seem to be milling around the public loos. Our waitress, following Bob's gaze as she sets down our teapot, kindly explains that they

are the last works of renowned Austrian-born artist, Friedrich Hundertwasser.
Commissioned in 1997, Hundertwasser, who made NZ his home in the 1970s, encouraged locals to take part: students crafted tiles and the windows were made from old bottles found in the neighbourhood. Intrigued, Bob photographs its mosaics while I queue with camera-toting tourists for a far more prosaic purpose!

We leave and drive along Paihia's waterfront, past families building castles in the sand, to the village proper where couples stroll hand in hand, and the squawking of gulls blends with laughter from its many cafés and bars.

After checking into our waterfront hotel, we enjoy an early dinner of fish and chips, seated – Paihia-style – on a park bench overlooking the water. Beady-eyed gulls observe our every move, while we in turn watch the bustling wharf from which vessels depart continuously: some ferry passengers to Russell, others carry dolphin-watchers or tour the bay's 144 islands en route to the Hole in the Rock.

As the sun sinks slowly into a blood-red sky, we walk across a long single-lane bridge to Waitangi, where NZ's founding document, the Treaty of Waitangi, was signed in 1840. By day it's a haunt for the historically-minded; by night it's the setting for a modern cultural production performed by a talented group of local Maori.

To Bob's delight, our guide, Kena Alexander, chooses him to act as our honorary 'chief'. As the light fades to dark we're greeted by a formidable band of warriors, but Bob (quietly quaking in his shoes) holds his ground to fulfill his chiefly obligations. Formalities completed, we're invited inside the Whare Runanga, where local tales unfold in a musical, narrated by an old Maori gentleman to his grandson. The whare depicts the ancestors of many Maori tribes in its intricate carvings including the great explorer Kupe, who landed in the Hokianga, on Northland's west coast.

Much later, aided by a glowing moon, we make our way back to Paihia and lulled by the gentle lapping of waves, drift off to sleep.

DAY TWO
Exploring the Bay of Islands – Paihia, Kerikeri and Russell

The soft early morning light brings showers. Water activities are off the agenda, but there are numerous other options. The vibrant township of Kerikeri seems inviting, so after a continental breakfast, we set off.

Half an hour later, rows of orange trees and mandarin groves hemmed with poplar indicate our arrival in this town, a haven for the gourmet traveller. From locally produced wine, olives and avocados, to cheese, ice cream and chocolate, there's something here to tempt everyone's taste buds.

Makana Confections is our first port of call and here we sample irresistible chocolate-dipped apricots and tantalisingly fresh citrus jellies – they taste as though they've just been picked from a tree! Bob leaves with a box of macadamia butter toffee crunch tucked under his arm, and we tour the workshops of talented artisans who craft a range of house-wares including kauri furniture, ceramics and even kaleidoscopes.

We peek into historic Kemp House (NZ's oldest-standing European building) and the Stone

Northland:
Attractions and Activities
Longview Winery: www.longviewwines.co.nz
Burning Issues: www.glass.co.nz/mahy.htm
Cultural Show: www.culturenorth.co.nz
Makana Confections: www.makana.co.nz
Kemp House: www.historic.org.nz
Excitor: www.excitor.co.nz
Drag netting: Mitimiti
Sand boarding: Opononi
Matakohe Kauri Museum: www.kauri-museum.com
Waiwera Hot Pools: www.waiwera.co.nz

Northland:
Cafés and Eateries
Riverside Café: Queen St, Warkworth
Trainspotting Café: Main Rd, Kawakawa
Cottle Hill Winery: SH10, Kerikeri
Kamakura: The Strand, Russell
Boatshed Café: 8 Clendon Esplanade, Rawene
Omapere Tourist Resort: SH12, Omapere
Funky Fish Café: 34 Seaview Rd, Baylys Beach

> " As the light fades to dark we're greeted by a formidable band of warriors "

Store, dating back to 1832, before doubling back past roadside stalls where I (to Bob's amazement) slip $5 into an honesty box in exchange for juicy oranges.

Passing Living Nature, where the fruits of Northland are used to produce natural skincare products, we arrive in time to lunch at Cottle Hill, on a sheltered terrace overlooking vines. A glass of Sailor's Delight Rosé teams well with an antipasto platter, and under Mike and Barbara Webb's guidance, we sample others from the vineyard's award-winning range.

Back in Paihia the sun's out so we jump aboard the Excitor, a thrillingly fast ride out to the Hole in the Rock via Russell, a round trip of an hour and a half. Bob spots a charter boat hunting for marlin, before we double back past Urupukapuka Island. Here we're joined by a pod of bottlenose dolphins that ride our bow waves to Moturua Island, where Captain Cook landed in 1769 to take on fresh water.

Bob and I take the option of disembarking in Russell, a quaint town full of historical buildings, each with its own colourful tale. We sit quietly for a time on its pebbled shores, trying hard to imagine the 1800s when this genteel settlement was overrun by whalers and deserting seamen, and earned its nickname, 'Hellhole of the Pacific'.

Today this couldn't be further from the truth. As the sun dips in the sky we walk along the waterline, then follow a bushwalk up to Flagstaff Hill where Hone Heke's warriors felled the British flag four times in protest of European settlers.

Suddenly a loud bell rings. "What on earth?" says Bob. We follow our ears to the wharf, where a charter boat has returned with a marlin. Locals and visitors alike mingle together as they await the weigh in; we retreat to Kamakura to dine on melt-in-the-mouth snapper beneath an orange-hued sunset before boarding a ferry back to Paihia.

DAY THREE
Paihia to Auckland via the Hokianga and Waipoua Forest

"Morning!" chirps Bob. We arise earlier on this, our last day, and travel across to the west coast and Rawene, a picturesque harbourside town located on the tip of a peninsula. There are many noteworthy buildings here, including Clendon House, but we make a beeline to The Boatshed Café. Built on stilts overhanging the harbour we breakfast on its terrace, watching mist rise from the mangroves as water laps gently beneath our seats.

A hoot from the vehicular ferry heralds its departure and we decide to take a side-trip, chugging across the Hokianga Harbour to Kohukohu. We drive through Panguru to the wild ocean beach at Mitimiti, where the misty peaks of the Warawara Forest roll down to meet the dunes.

And here – by fortune or design – we meet a local man, Tipo Cash. He shows us around his marae and onto the beach sharing riveting stories about the chief who was killed on a rock giving Mitimiti its name, the graves of Chinese flax workers in the dunes, and

Opua - Deerace Publishing

legends of the Waitaha.

A keen fisherman, Tipo reckons drag netting for mullet using traditional methods is the most popular activity in these parts. "Have a go," he urges, but instead we help gather mussels off the rocks for the elders.

Back in Rawene we drive to Opononi, the home of Opo, a young, friendly bottle-nosed dolphin who adopted the town and played with children during the summer of 1955-56. A committee was set up to safeguard her while regulations for the protection of dolphins were passed into law. In a tragic twist, Opo was found dead in a pool the following day, jammed between a cleft in the rocks.

Today all that remains is a stone memorial opposite the wharf and some old film footage at the museum. A group of locals gathers outside the Four Square store. They tell us the fishing has been good of late and ask if we'd like to try sand boarding. We choose to watch from the wharf as kids and backpackers cart old body boards up giant dunes and ride them down, landing with a splash in the harbour.

In Omapere a viewing area provides a last glimpse of the harbour, before entering Waipoua Forest. We pass the visitors centre and numerous hikes but decide to make only one stop en route: to pay our respects to Tane Mahuta, the largest kauri of all. A five-minute walk, alive with birdsong, leads us through bush to this enormous kauri tree, and we sit in silence beneath, revelling in its sheer magnificence. Estimated to be around 2000 years old, Tane Mahuta is one of several notable kauri trees in the forest.

Further south we skip the Kai Iwi Lakes in favour of lunch at Baylys Beach. Here we relax at the Funky Fish Café, surrounded by sculpture and original art works, tapping our feet in time to 88.2 FM, a radio station operating from a local's shed. Its reception is only one kilometre but that's more than enough coverage for the folk surfcasting from the beach.

Refreshed we continue to Dargaville and to Ruawai through flats lush with kumara crops.

In Matakohe we stop to stretch our legs at the Kauri Museum and lose ourselves for a while in days of old: a rugged world of kauri-felling, gum digging and hardy pioneers. For a time Bob disappears; I find him stroking a giant piece of kauri gum with an amber-glint in his eye.

At the antiques store in Paparoa we join the locals in sifting for treasures. Bob discovers a nice souvenir - a translucent piece of gum.

East of Maungaturoto, SH12 meets SH1 and we return south to Wellsford. Caught up in my own lecture on the hardships of the gum digging days, I miss the alternate route to Auckland via Helensville.

And my co-pilot? Well he's on auto, having stashed our map in the glovebox along with his shells, chocolates and kauri gum. Somewhere near Puhoi I think I smell sulphur from the Waiwera Hot Pools but it turns out it's Bob's now-reeking crab's claw. Luckily it's a well-timed reminder as there's no finer way to end a day. We relax in hot thermal pools before returning to the glittering lights of the city. ■

Cape Reinga is a place of great spiritual significance to Maori. They believe it is "the place of the leaping", where the souls of the dead gather before they enter the next world. According to Maori traditions the spirits of the departed leap from an 800-year-old pohutukawa tree on the windswept cape to begin the voyage back to their final resting place in the ancestral homeland of Hawaiki.

The passage to the afterlife begins at Te-oneroa-o-tohe, known as Ninety Mile Beach. Spirits travel the length of the beach carrying a regional token such as a fern frond or manuka cutting. These offerings are placed on Te Arai Rock near the Bluff and the journey continues inland at Twilight Beach towards Cape Reinga, and crosses a stream. Those who choose not to drink from the stream return to the body, while those who choose to quench their thirst continue on to the gnarled pohutukawa tree and leap, descending through its tangled roots, to the sea bed. From here they travel to Ohau Island, the largest of the Three Kings Islands, where they resurface and bid Aotearoa (New Zealand) farewell before returning home. A clear day at Cape Reinga offers powerful views. The Three Kings Islands, named by Abel Tasman in 1643, are visible on the horizon while spectacular Cape Maria Van Diemen dominates the west. To the east the long curve of Spirits Bay leads the eye to the dark smudge of the North Cape. Directly ahead, the towering breakers of the Tasman Sea and the Pacific Ocean collide in a maelstrom of churning waves and spume.

Several fine coastal walks depart from Cape Reinga. Cape Maria Van Diemen is reached via the golden stretch of Te Werahi Beach, while to the east a track leads to Tapotupotu Bay - a popular camping and picnicking spot - and on to Spirits Bay.

CAPE REINGA

The site of the legendary money tree, where early settlers travelling north left an offering to ward off evil spirits, is reached via a route further south.

A trip to the cape is not complete without travelling one-way via Ninety Mile Beach's sand highway, entering or exiting on Te Paki Stream. This magnificent beach arches in an unbroken stretch of white sand for some 103 km (64 miles). The European name is something of a misnomer, its length possibly having been originally recorded in kilometres from Ahipara. Shells from the rare toheroa, a type of clam that grows to 150 mm in length, are often found by beachcombers, while its smaller (and more plentiful) cousin the tuatua is gathered by locals and minced to make delicious tuatua fritters and nourishing soup.
The beach is flanked by the Aupouri Forest, and here wild horses roam. Some folks believe these fine-looking horses are the progeny of thoroughbreds that escaped a ship wrecked off nearby Cape Maria Van Diemen.

On the east coast a white sand dune containing some of the world's purest silica marks the entrance to Parengarenga Harbour. Godwits gather here in early March and, when the dune is almost black with their sheer numbers, they take off on their annual migration to Siberia and Alaska.

The old gumdigging town of Houhora hosts a legendary annual hunt: locals compete to catch one pig, one duck, one pheasant, one trevally and one snapper - all on the same day! The Houhora Tavern housed inside an old woolshed is a good venue to meet hardy northlanders, while the Subritsky Homestead, built in 1860 from local materials and plastered with a powdered seashell paste, provides a fascinating glimpse into the past.

At the Ancient Kauri Kingdom in Awanui, swamp kauri logs dating from 30,000 to 50,000 years ago are crafted into furniture and house-wares, while Paparore's Gumdiggers Park offers further insight into the world of gumdiggers with its authentic 100-year-old gumfield and buried forest. Here the remains of two kauri forests, felled by unknown catastrophic events between 42,000 and 150,000 years ago, are buried beneath gumdigger's holes.

The round trip to Cape Reinga can be completed on an independent day-trip from Paihia. Alternatively a number of operators provide coach and 4wd tours ex-Paihia and as rental cars are not permitted to be driven on Ninety Mile Beach we recommend taking a tour. Most drive one-way via Ninety Mile Beach and return by road. ■

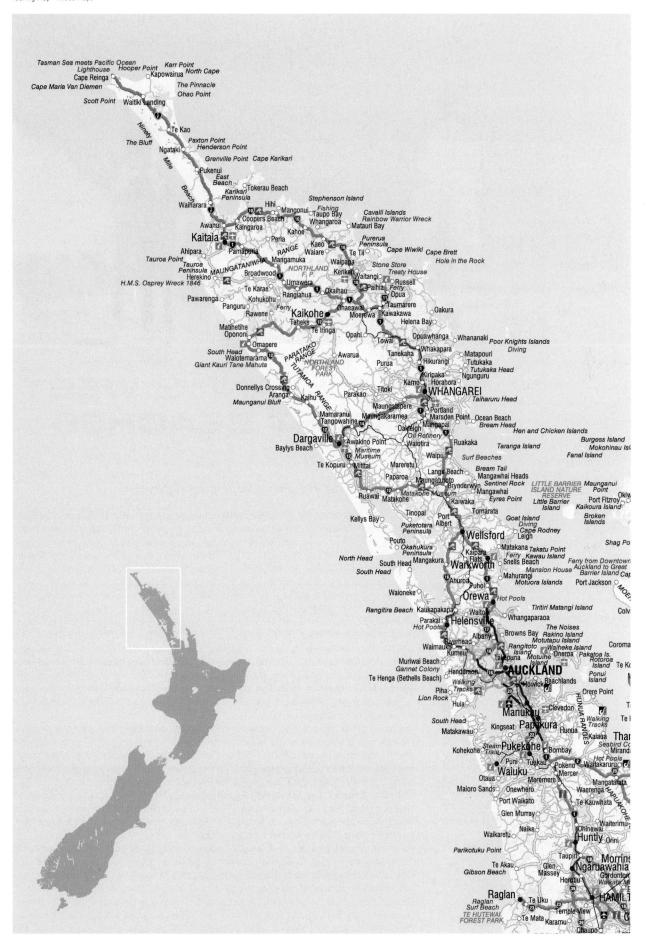

AUCKLAND'S **WEST COAST BEACHES**

Well-known for its wineries, gannets, black sands and dramatic scenery, the West Coast of Auckland offers visitors the opportunity to see another side of the City of Sails. The Waitakere Ranges dominate this region and were formed by a series of volcanic eruptions. Today the ranges are covered in dense rainforest, which receives around forty percent more rain than Auckland City. Many of its rivers are dammed to form large reservoirs that hold the water consumed by the city below.

Its wild, rugged coastline has a raw natural beauty, which tends to attract artistic types and those who endorse strong environmental principles, while its scenery has provided a backdrop for many award-winning movies - including *The Piano* - and popular TV series.

We head west to soak up the atmosphere, surf its breakers, ride horses on the beach, taste wine, admire gannets and meet the locals.

DAY ONE
Auckland to Piha with a side trip to Whatipu

High in the foothills of the Waitakere Ranges the elevated township of Titirangi is reached via the North Western Motorway. We arrive ready to breakfast and follow our noses to the German café, Boss Konditorei, where fresh organic and wholegrain breads are baked daily. Its street appeal isn't up to much and Bob screws up his nose, but once inside the views of the Manukau Harbour and selection of specialty cakes and breads win him over and he winds up telling its friendly owner, Ewald Boss, that he intends to return for lunch.

Instead we purchase a selection of thick-cut sandwiches and pastries so we can picnic at our leisure, then visit the art gallery at Lopdell House where locals exhibit their work. As we leave Bob strikes up a conversation with a student-type with gorgeous long red locks. Her T-shirt states "Titirangi – it's the west...but with a special flavour all its own. Titirangi is more than a village; it's a way of living; it's a feeling – it's a state of mind." She tells Bob to get out to Whatipu, "You won't believe you're in Auckland," and departs to the local hairdressing salon, where all the products used are organic.

And so we take the road to Whatipu, past popular Cornwallis Beach with its icecream and coffee caravan, the bottle-green horseshoe of Huia Bay and over the hills to Whatipu, nestled amongst the dunes.

The boom of the ocean can be heard from the carpark and it becomes thunderous as we walk along a sandy pathway lined with colourful flowering grasses to the beach. Here surf pounds relentlessly against Paratutae Island which marks the northern head of the Manukau Harbour. It was the site of one of NZ's most disastrous shipwrecks in 1863, when the HMS Orpheus ran aground at the cost of 189 lives.

I lead Bob along a rough unmarked route to the sea caves that were used in early days as shelter by local Maori, and later - in the 1920s - as a ballroom for timber workers. We pass Whatipu Lodge, built for the mill manager in 1867, and Liebergreen Cottage, a former mill workers cottage, thought to date from the 1860s.

We picnic amongst the dunes in swaying grasses watching the surf pound in. Bob reminisces about a surfing holiday he once had in Hawaii and how he was a dab hand on a Malibu board. As I watch him gobble pastries it's pretty hard to imagine but I simply suggest that he hires a board and gives it a go.

There are no surfers at Whatipu today because the waves and currents are too dangerous, so we return to Titirangi and turn off onto Scenic Drive. It travels through the heart of the Waitakere Ranges which are cloaked in some 16,000 hectares of native rainforest, and feature waterfalls and several popular black sand surf beaches including Karekare, Piha,

Bethells and Muriwai Beach.

The Arataki Visitor's Centre is our next port of call, a good starting point for any exploration of this region. There's a plant identification trail giving a good insight into local flora, and inside a range of displays outlines everything from the history of the region to short biographies on local artists. Bob spends quite some time admiring the sweeping views of Nihotapu Dam and Manukau Harbour from its back decks.

A huge volcano formed the Waitakeres over 20 million years ago, and today we can still see many large kauri, rimu and kahikatea trees. Kauri was logged here in the early 1800s and there are several tramways in the bush that were originally used for the logging industry. Later they provided access for workers to construct dams and waterpipes and more recently transport sightseers aboard Watercare's Rainforest Express to view the Upper Nihotupu Dam.

As we continue along Scenic Drive there are numbers of points offering panoramic views of Auckland Harbour Bridge, the Sky Tower and beyond to Rangitoto and Waiheke Island. We stop several times before turning off to Piha and checking into our accommodation, an original kiwi bach (holiday home) overlooking the water.

It's late afternoon and as the sun drops in the sky, Bob decides to try his hand surfcasting using a rod from the bach. "I'll be back soon with fish," he calls out as I leave, shaking my head, to pick up supplies from the Piha Store.

Outside I meet a man on the verandah painting a picture of Lion Rock, a massive island-like rock which sprouts from the middle of the beach. We chat for a while and it's almost dark by the time I return to our abode armed with breakfast supplies, fresh bread and a can of baked beans for dinner.

"Oh ye of little faith," says Bob later on as he fries a decent sized snapper which we eat seated upon deck chairs on the verandah and watch the sun set.

DAY TWO
Piha to Muriwai and Waimauku

The next morning, fired up from his successful fishing expedition, Bob announces that it's a good day to surf. Because Auckland's West Coast beaches are notoriously dangerous I suggest that perhaps he's a little rusty and may benefit from a quick refresher at Muriwai's acclaimed surf school. Besides, I say, cementing the deal, I want to go horseriding on Muriwai beach.

We set off and complete the final leg of Scenic Drive, then drive through pretty countryside to Muriwai village. A sign outside the surf shop states there's a 3-5ft swell and an onshore breeze. "It's all good," says Bob (an expression picked up from yesterday's redhead), as I leave and drive along to the horse park to meet up with the crew at Muriwai Beach Horseriding. Here, as a beginner, I'm carefully matched with my mount: a gentle yet tough station-bred horse named Sherman, who plods sedately along the long black beach and back through the iron-rich dunes.

The sand is the result of eroded rock, rich in iron ore spewed from Mt Taranaki and washed north by strong currents. Light as dust, it sticks like glue to your skin and can sometimes be found for days after a visit to the beach. Brushing it off as best I can I return to collect Bob from the Surf School.

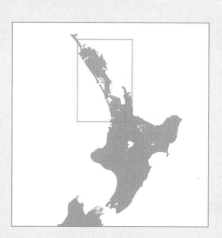

West Auckland:
Attractions and Activities

Lopdell House: www.lopdell.org.nz
Arataki Visitors Centre: Scenic Drive, Titirangi
Muriwai Surf School: www.muriwaisurfschool.co.nz
Muriwai Beach Horseriding: www.aucklandhorsehire.org.nz
Matua Valley Wines: www.matua.co.nz
4TRACK Adventures: www.4trackadventures.co.nz
Tree Adventures: www.tree-adventures.com
BeesOnline: www.beesOnline.co.nz
4WD Adventures: www.extreme4wd.co.nz
Canyoning: awoladventures.co.nz

West Auckland:
Cafés and Eateries

Boss Konditorei: 410 Titirangi Rd, Titirangi
Hardware Café: 404 Titirangi Rd, Titirangi
Waterfront Café: 409 Motutara Rd, Muriwai
Hunting Lodge: Waikoukou Valley Rd, Waimaukau
BeesOnline: 791 SH16, Waimaukau
Muriwai Pizza Garage: 290 Oaia Rd, Muriwai
Soljans Estate Winery: 366 SH16, Kumeu

> "We picnic amongst the dunes in swaying grasses watching the surf pound in"

"He's a bit of a legend on the Malibu," says the young instructor, giving me a wink as we leave. Over a burger lunch at Muriwai's casual Waterfront Café we exchange notes before heading up the hill to visit the Takapu Gannet Colony.

Here these magnificent birds nest on large rocky plateaus in the cliffs and we wander along cliff top tracks where interpretative display boards describe the gannets' lifestyle including their feeding habits and rearing of young. The colony, which has grown steadily since the 1970s, boasts hundreds of birds and we watch as they take off using strong updrafts to help them aloft on wings spanning up to two metres.

We then drive to Waimauku to enjoy a wine tasting at Matua Valley Winery, where the Spence brothers pioneered New Zealand's first Sauvignon Blanc. Their wide range of distinctive wines includes the Matua Valley's Ararimu Chardonnay 2000, which was pronounced the best chardonnay at the International Wine and Spirit Competition in London for its excellent varietal characteristics and well-judged sense of oak.

During our relaxed yet informed tasting, Bob chats with Bill Spence about the best surfcasting possies on the west coast. Much to my amusement, last night's catch grows substantially larger in size as we work through the wines on offer.

Tired yet strangely refreshed from our adventurous day, we decide to stay at Vineyard Cottages. We check in early and spend the remainder of the afternoon relaxing on the verandah beneath a roof of thick grapevines.

Later, armed with a torch, we make our way through the vineyard to dine at the Hunting Lodge Restaurant, housed inside a 130-year-old cottage. I enjoy a thick game broth, followed by seared ostrich; Bob indulges in scallops followed by a juicy venison steak. Wearily we return to our cottage and turn in; Bob dreams of catching an immense fish, while I soar like a gannet above thunderous surf.

DAY THREE
Return to Auckland city

We welcome a slow start in the morning, breakfasting upon bacon, eggs, tomatoes, mushrooms and a crusty loaf from the provided self-cook basket. For a time we enjoy soaking up the rays from the morning sun on the patio at the back of the cottage, before we drive to Woodhill Forest. The production forest – all 12,500 hectares of it – provides a range of outdoor adventure activities. From quad biking to four wheel driving, horseriding, clay bird shooting, hiking, off-road motorcycling and mountain biking, there's something here for everyone.

Bob and I choose to go our own ways again as he's keen to learn to ride a quad bike. While he trains on 4-Track Adventures' practice circuit under the expert instruction of Dan Ireland, and then joy-rides his way through muddy pools and forest streams to the beach, I hike to a sign-posted lookout. It offers good views of the forest, and after watching horses depart on the popular Woodhill Forest Horse Trail, I challenge myself on the rope courses at the

Gannets at Muriwai - Donna Blaber

Woodhill Tree Adventure Park. The first of its kind in NZ, there are eight courses to complete, ranging from easy to difficult. There's no age restriction as your height determines whether or not you're able to do a course. If you measure more than 1.40 metres you can do them all! I get through five before chickening out and after watching others complete the course I depart to pick up Bob.

He sits in the sun wearing facial mud splashes like a badge of honour and he's talking to Tom, an outdoorsy bloke with whom he's obviously struck up quite a rapport about – you guessed it – fishing.. "I reckon the best surfcasting is from Bethells," says Tom. "I'm heading out there later this arvo," he adds as we leave.

"Where's Bethells Beach?" enquires Bob, ferreting around in the glovebox for the map.

Back in Waimauku we stop for lunch at BeesOnline, an organically certified and GE free honey centre, watching bees through a two-storey glass theatre as we dine. I try their delicious courgette, fennel and tuatua fritters served with honey wasabi mayo and a garden herb salad, while Bob enjoys the hot vegetable wedge mix with honey mustard mayonnaise.

After lunch we browse through the shop, where the honey and bee products for sale range from honeygar (honey-flavoured vinegar), to Bee Pollen, honey soap and candles. Bob picks up a golden bottle of White Wine and Clover Honeygar, "It'll be tasty on my next snapper," he says.

We drive to Kumeu where a wealth of orchards and vineyards reflect the town's Yugoslavian heritage, and a mix of vineyards offer a diverse range of wine styles. Some are made from locally grown grapes, while others are produced from grapes grown in Marlborough, Hawkes Bay, Gisborne and Wairarapa.

We call into Kerr Farm Vineyard, a small boutique vineyard specialising in Kumeu varietals, and sample wine seated at a large oak table with owners Jaison and Wendy Kerr, then we visit Soljans Estate, Coopers Creek and Kumeu River, filling up the boot with bottles of wine as we go.

At 4 pm I indicate for Auckland, then having second thoughts, I turn to Bob. "Want to meet up with Tom at Bethells?" I ask, grinning as his face lights up.

"Sure do," he replies, grabbing the map off the dash, "and I know just how to get there!" ■

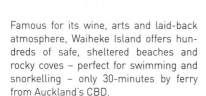

Famous for its wine, arts and laid-back atmosphere, Waiheke Island offers hundreds of safe, sheltered beaches and rocky coves – perfect for swimming and snorkelling – only 30-minutes by ferry from Auckland's CBD.

The island is a heady mix of the old and the new, a place where architecturally designed mansions and salty holiday homes mingle in a jumbled seaside manner. The same works for clothes, and although bare feet, jandals, tank tops and shorts are standard attire, practically anything goes.

Many artists live on Waiheke and their creativity and influence is reflected in all spheres of island life. A laid-back atmosphere permeates and no matter where you are, life revolves around the beach. There are many coves to choose from and several days could be spent simply exploring the coastline: Oneroa with its golden sand and calm waters, picturesque Enclosure Bay, and the pretty curve of Palm Beach.

Onetangi, with its light surf and stunning views north to Little Barrier Island, is a popular place to hang out. Relax on its white sand, take a dip in the crystal-clear ocean, or - if you've ever wondered what it's like to swoop like a seagull - try paragliding with Seabirds. A speedboat pulls punters aloft from the beach and the towline is released at 2000 feet, so you can glide back down to the beach.

Other popular waterbased activities include kayaking, sailing and windsurfing. From October through to March, Marc Kampschulte of Windsurfing Waiheke sets up his windsurfing trailer at Surfdale, while Dawn Perkins of The Kayak Company provides kayak tuition, rentals, and half-day or full-day tours to beaches with no road access.

WAIHEKE ISLAND

Waiheke Island has long been a yachtie's paradise, and many boats pull into its sheltered bays and deep inlets to anchor at night, including Bernard Rhodes and his son, Andrew - who offer sailing trips aboard *Flying Carpet:* an ocean-going, bi-plane-rigged catamaran. Sailing on the *Flying Carpet* is a relaxed affair: most guests relax and enjoy the scenery, but keen sailors are welcome to help trim the sails.

Whilst Waiheke's nature trails, art trails, shady olive groves, sculpture gardens and range of modern eateries are tempting, it's the island's vineyards that provide the greatest drawcard.

At the Tuscan-style villa of Stonyridge, Norton, a sizeable black Labrador wearing a collar saying: "Do not feed me," greets visitors. A heavy wooden doorway leads to the winery's café overlooking grapevines and olive trees. Wide doors open to a sunny, sheltered courtyard cobbled with stones and shells; leafy vines twist around pergola poles, and Boston ivy creeps up the adobe walls. The food is superb, the wine outstanding (this is the home of NZ's most sought-after red), and the setting stylish yet casual, with a relaxed Mediterranean country atmosphere.

This vineyard, along with Goldwater Estate, was the first to plant grapes on Waiheke Island, and when both proved successful, many others followed suit. Today there's a wide range to visit including Kennedy Point Vineyard, which produces delicious Sauvignon Blanc (best teamed with an antipasto platter and sampled on its shady pohutukawa-fringed decks); Te Whau Vineyard with its extensive wine list and spectacular views of Auckland city from Te Whau Point; and Onetangi Vineyard, next to Stonyridge, where you can also sample locally brewed Baroona beer.

There's also a wealth of popular cafés and vineyard restaurants including the Mudbrick Café, a popular haunt for visiting Aucklanders with its stunning city views, and Salvage, Schooner and Vino Vino in Oneroa.

For an entertaining night out Waiheke-style, join the locals and curl up on family-donated couches at the community cinema in Oneroa. It's perfectly kosher to take along a bottle of your favourite red, and grab a curry from Ajadz next door to enjoy while watching the movie!

Fullers Ferries runs an hourly service to the island from the Ferry Terminal opposite Queen Elizabeth Square in downtown Auckland. The ferry ride takes 35 – 45 minutes. Some ferries travel via Devonport and/or Rangitoto Island. If you wish to take your car across Subritzky Sealink offer a vehicular ferry service from Half Moon Bay. Flights to Waiheke Island are also available from Auckland airport. ▓

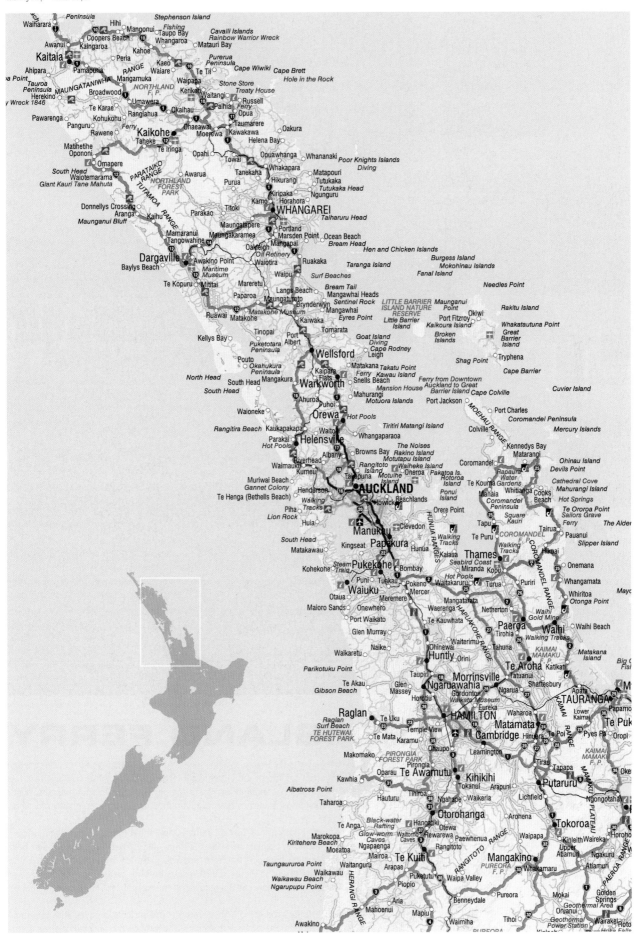

THE INTER-ISLAND FERRY

Cruise across Cook Strait on one of the inter-island ferries and enjoy the scenery from the comfort of one of their many observation decks. It's the perfect place to spot dolphins, seals and many kinds of seabirds on a journey that rates amongst the most scenic ferry crossings in the world.

Cook Strait was named in memory of Captain James Cook, the intrepid explorer who discovered in 1770 that - contrary to popular belief at the time - NZ is made up of two major land masses. The inter-island ferry connects the North and South Islands of New Zealand travelling from Wellington, NZ's capital city, to Picton, a picturesque harbour town located at the head of the Queen Charlotte Sound and known as the gateway to the magnificent Marlborough Sounds and the South Island of NZ.

The scenic ferry journey offers many highlights en route and is richly supplied with local legends and myths. From Wellington, the ferry makes its way through the harbour offering panoramic views of its dramatic cityscape set on high hills which plunge steeply into the sea. It

The inter-island ferries provide scheduled services across the Cook Strait for passengers, vehicles, commercial vehicles and rail freight, and links New Zealand's North and South Islands. There are normally 3-4 sailings per day in each direction, however the frequency and departure times of sailings do change from season to season, so be sure to check up-to-date timetables.

The ferry terminal in Wellington is located on Aotea Quay, five minutes north of the Wellington Railway Station, and is open daily from 7 am until 7 pm; and Monday to Friday 10.30 pm to 1.30 am. A free shuttle bus is provided from platform 9 at the Wellington Railway Station.

The ferry terminal in Picton is located on Auckland Street in central Picton and is open Tuesday to Sunday from 4.30 am to 9.30 pm, and on Mondays from 8 am to 9.30 am.

If you are holidaying in New Zealand during the height of summer, from December through to February, it is advisable to book your tickets at least two weeks in advance.

Limited places are available in the private club lounges and so should be reserved at the same time that you make your advance booking. For further ferry information please refer to www.ferrytickets.co.nz or free-phone 0800 500 660 (within NZ). From outside NZ, please call +64 3 379 1451.

travels past Ward Island in Wellington Harbour, which according to Maori legend is one of the daughters of the great Polynesian explorer Kupe, and then past Somes Island, used as a detention centre during WWII. At the entrance to the Wellington Harbour it skims Pencarrow Head, the site of NZ's oldest lighthouse (built in 1859) and around the point to Oterangi Bay, the North Island terminal of the Cook Strait power cable and the place where in April 1968 a land wind speed of 268 km/h was recorded, then out into Cook Strait. From here passengers are offered fantastic views of the South Island's Kaikoura Range and there are frequent opportunities to spot dolphins and sea birds.

One third of the journey involves cruising through the majestic Marlborough Sounds, a series of sunken sea-filled valleys that feature many bush clad islands, hidden inlets and bays, clear waters and native forests growing down to the waterline, with glimpses of small wooden homes, jetties and boatsheds owned by locals, many of whom commute via the water.

On some ferries, for a small additional charge, a private 'club' lounge is available and provides a peaceful setting to unwind. It offers complimentary tea and coffee, juices and cookies, plus daily newspapers and current magazines.

A food court, café/bar, children's corner, shops and work stations are also provided for passengers' comfort and convenience. ■

The Coromandel Peninsula is one of NZ's most-loved holiday destinations. Its spectacular coastline provides a mix of sandy bays and rocky coves, while the rugged, volcanic backbone is cloaked in a dense robe of native forest and boasts some of NZ's best hiking. From the old gold mining town of Coromandel, with its laid-back artisan community, across to Mercury Bay's magnificent Cathedral Cove on the east coast and south to Whakatane and the Bay of Plenty, visitors will find a region with a rich gold mining history and a wide range of activities to enjoy.

We take a three-day drive and visit a migratory bird sanctuary, discover old gold mines and stamper batteries, hunt for flounder, call in to visit local potters and artisans at their home studios and take a life-changing trip to the live marine volcano of White Island off the coast of Whakatane.

AUCKLAND TO
WHAKATANE

DAY ONE
Auckland to Coromandel Town

Leaving Auckland we drive south through Clevedon to the Seabird Coast. The road travels alongside the still waters and startling-white shell banks of the Firth of Thames from Kaiaua to Miranda with its world-renowned, 8500-hectare, intertidal sanctuary for migratory birds.
We stop at the Miranda Shorebird Centre, where detailed display boards explain how the region is a temporary abode for thousands of migrating shorebirds navigating their way from Eastern Siberia and the Alaskan tundra to spend the summer in New Zealand.
The bar-tailed godwit and lesser knot are the most commonly sighted tourists.
"It's a long way to come for a little R&R," jokes Bob, as we stand on the shoreline scouting for birds. There are hundreds including pied oyster-catchers who return to the Firth after breeding in the South Island.
We drive past the popular Miranda Hot Springs, where the waters of these once swamp-like natural springs were transformed in 1959 into what was then the largest thermal pool in the Southern Hemisphere, and on to Waitakaruru where two one-way bridges pass over the same river.
Stretching our legs in the Waitakaruru antique store, we hear from an old-timer that the army built the second bridge for the Queen's visit to New Zealand in 1953. "Up in a day," he grumbles, "Don't see that now!"
A long, single-lane bridge leads to Kopu and ten minutes later we're in Thames, a town that had a larger population than Auckland back in the height of the 1880s gold boom. There are a number of old buildings and relics from that era, particularly at its northern end around Grahamstown.
We pop into Eco People, with its dazzling array of hand-crafted soaps. One novel product is 'Washy Squashy' moulding soap; it's similar to kids' play dough, but easier on the clothes and home. Some of the soap, like the blackberry, sweet kiwifruit, feijoa and mandarin bars, smell almost edible and I keep an eye on Bob - when it comes to him and food, nothing would surprise me!
In Tararu we park on the quiet shore and enjoy a cup of thermos tea, then continue north. Our route takes us through contorted pohutukawa trees growing so thickly on the cliffs that the telephone lines must leave the bank and journey across the water.
A steep hill provides superb views of the Coromandel Peninsula, the Firth of Thames and Auckland hiding behind Ponui and Waiheke Islands. We descend to Coromandel Town, home to around 1400 keen boaties, conservationists, lifestylers and craftspeople.
Strolling around town, Bob's kept busy taking snapshots of the fine Victorian buildings and

Paku Hill, Tairua- Tourism Coromandel

Karangahake Gorge - Tourism Coromandel

relics from the gold mining and timber industries. We call into Weta, the Source and Art Xtreme, where local artisans display their wares.

Over paninis at Success Café, we decide to spend the afternoon taking a train ride at Driving Creek Railway, and soaking up local history at the Coromandel Stamper Battery. When we arrive, Bob's amazed by the size of the river-powered waterwheel standing 7.5 metres high. Ashley Franklyn shows us around. "Gold was discovered at Driving Creek in 1852 and the battery was erected in 1898 to determine the quality of ore," he says, demonstrating how it works and answering our many questions.

"There's not much he doesn't know about gold mining in this town," says Bob as we leave and drive the short distance to Driving Creek Railway, a 27-year-old project that is still evolving under the direction of Barry Brickell, a highly creative potter.

Fortunately we get to meet Barry himself, a colourful local character. He tells us that he never intended his railway to become a tourist attraction and that the first sections of track were built to gain all-weather access to the clay.

We hop aboard and with a toot we're off, chugging along a narrow-gauge 15-inch track, which winds up the hills behind the potteries. There are tunnels, spirals, and a double-decker viaduct en route and the track zigzags its way up the hill to Barry's latest creation, the 'Eyeful Tower', a wooden terminus providing truly eye-popping views of the Coromandel.

Later we check in to our accommodation for the night, a self contained kauri cottage built in the 1850s, and dine on bowls of freshly steamed green-lipped mussels – the kai moana (seafood) for which Coromandel Town is renowned.

We finish our evening at the beach where locals are hunting for flounder by flashlight. They lend us some gear – a couple of torches and knives strapped to sticks of manuka – and we slowly wade through the water looking for the telltale outlines in the sand of these flat fish. I spear the first and Bob (ever the great fisherman) races over to help get it into the bag. Shortly after there's a loud whoop and he scores another. We thank our newfound friends and head home with our breakfast.

DAY TWO
Coromandel Town to Whangamata

A tree outside the cottage provides a lemon in the morning. After a sumptuous feed we decide to skip SH25 in favour of the 309 Road and the Waiau Waterworks. We depart, but first call into the Coromandel Smoking Company where we pick up hot smoked trevally for our picnic basket.

At the Waiau Waterworks we find creative feats of engineering and large sculptures sprawling over the Ogilvie's four-and-a-half acres.

"I've always wanted to do silly things with water," says Chris Ogilvie when we arrive. We walk through its gardens beside the Waiau River and there are several fun rides, all of which are powered by water, plus a variety of water-powered clocks, butter churns, waterwheels and intriguing pedal-powered pumps. Feeling energetic Bob takes a ride on the Flying Fox, which like many of the Waterworks creations, is made from recycled materials – it even includes brake calipers from an old car.

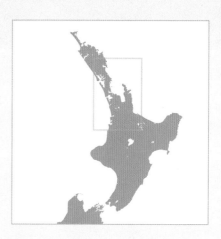

Auckland to Whakatane:
Attractions and Activities

Shorebird Centre: www.miranda-shorebird.org.nz
Miranda Hot Springs: Miranda
Eco People: www.ecopeople.co.nz
Driving Creek Railway: www.drivingcreekrailway.co.nz
Coromandel Stamper Battery: Coromandel Town
Waiau Waterworks: www.waiauwaterworks.co.nz
Cathedral Cove Kayaking: www.seakayaktours.co.nz
Hahei Explorer: www.haheiexplorer.co.nz
Waihi Goldmining Museum: www.waihimuseum.co.nz
White Island Tours: www.whiteisland.co.nz

Auckland to Whakatane:
Cafés and Eateries

Success Café: Kapanga Rd, Coromandel Town
Coro Takeaways: 124 Wharf Rd, Coromandel Town
Pepper Tree Restaurant: Kapanga Rd, Coromandel Town
Admirals Arms: 146 Wharf Rd, Coromandel Town
Colenso Café: SH25, Whenuakite
Coast Restaurant: 501 Port Rd, Whangamata
Oceanas: 328 Ocean Rd, Whangamata

Mussel Farm Coromandel Harbour - Toursim Coromandel
below: Hot Water Beach - Donna Blaber

White Island - Tourism Bay of Plenty
below: Driving Creek Railway - Donna Blaber

> "The ground shudders beneath our feet, hissing and groaning as we follow our guide across a stony, lunar-like landscape"

We leave and drive across the peninsula past the Waiau Falls and Coromandel Forest Park before rejoining SH25.

A ten kilometre drive north leads to Whitianga, the main hub for marine-based activities departing for the Te Whanganui A Hei Marine Reserve, which stretches from Cooks Bluff and Motukoruro Island through to Mahurangi Island. But we head south as you can also access this park from Hahei.

En route we call into the roadside Wilderland Organic Shop and fill our picnic basket with ripe avocados and delicious peppery rocket.

In Hahei we join Nigel Horne's Hahei Explorer and cruise to Cathedral Cove, where a gigantic arched cavern penetrates the headland and forms an arch. Hidden beneath the waves are many other similar structures, which shelter unique marine life and plants.

We continue south to explore the Orua sea cave. Bob gets a fright when a large drop of icy water lands on his forehead, but Nigel assures him that this is considered good luck by local Maori.

Duly blessed, we return to Hahei and drive to Hot Water Beach.

We eat our picnic sitting on the beach watching people dig holes in the sand. Then we dig our own private pool and wallow in its warm thermal waters until the tide begins to turn.

In Whenuakite we visit Alan Rhodes's eco-friendly potting community where potter Bobby Neal shows us around. Clay is dug onsite and pottery wares are created using a variety of firing methods. Bob adds a blue butter dish to his collection of purchases, which are now housed in a box in the boot.

We drive to Mt Paku in Tairua, and take a short hike to the top. From here we have outstanding 360-degree views of Tairua's harbour and the long sprawl of holiday homes at Pauanui. Maori legend has it that if you climb to the top of Paku, you'll return here within seven years. Bob's more than happy with this arrangement but wonders out loud if they'll also shout him a ticket.

We cross the one-lane bridge at the southern end of Tairua and head south through the Tairua Forest, turning off at Opoutere. A ten minute hike through pines leads to its broad sweep of sand and we complete a loop through the Wharekawa Harbour Wildlife Refuge, where NZ dotterel and variable oyster-catchers breed, back to the carpark.

As we leave Bob spots a sign for Topadahil Studios, and we drive up a long steep driveway to meet artist Guity Evelyn. Her paintings explore light, colour and depth, and have an incredible energy and warmth. I pick up a framed print entitled 'Moon Glow' for $25, before we continue on to Whangamata to check into a B&B.

A popular surfing resort and more recently a favoured place to retire, Whangamata provides many good cafés and restaurants including The Coast, The Bach and Oceana's Restaurant. We head to the latter and enjoy an early dinner of delicious pan-fried gurnard with a salmon and dill sauce, sautéed potatoes and bowls of fresh salad greens.

Later we return to our B&B via Whangamata's beautiful white sandy beach and are lulled to sleep by the sound of waves breaking on the shore.

DAY THREE
Whangamata to Whakatane

After a light continental breakfast inhouse we depart and drive to Waihi, an old mining town where gold bearing quartz was discovered in 1878. There are many quaint buildings lining Waihi's main street, including several old miners' cottages. We stop for lattés at an antiquated coffee shop and discover that gold and silver production still continues at the Martha Mine, but it's hidden well from view.

Interest piqued, we explore the town's colourful past at the Waihi Gold Mining Museum and Arts Centre, then climb aboard a vintage train which puffs its way along these historic tracks to Waikino station, where the Victoria Battery began its ear-splitting work in 1896.

Returning to Waihi we leave town and travel south on SH2 to Katikati, driving alongside the harbour to Tauranga. Here we order a delicious wood-fired pizza for lunch at Mills Reef Winery before continuing south on SH2 to Te Puke, where the NZ kiwifruit industry had its beginnings.

Outside Longridge Park we debate whether to take a guided tour of a working kiwifruit farm. We choose instead to continue to Whakatane and join a tour to White Island, an active volcano which puffs and splutters endless tons of sulphur dioxide into the atmosphere, some 49 kilometres off the coast.

On the wharf we join 16 others and board *Pee Jay*, a luxury launch purpose-built for the journey. We're thrilled when hundreds of bottlenose dolphins join us for the ride, merrily ducking and dancing on the bow waves.

Under the charred silhouette of White Island we don hard hats and - gas masks swinging at the ready - board the inflatable and disembark on White Island's formidable terrain.

Many visitors turn back on arrival and Bob is in awe as we trek past the grotesque blistered remains of the old sulphur mine rising from the ashes.

The ground shudders beneath our feet, groaning as we follow our guide across a stony, lunar-like landscape. Jagged red ridges rise above vivid coppery-yellow fumaroles that discharge gas under such pressure that it roars through holes in the ground like a squadron of B52 bombers, its choking emissions surging in cumulus formations across the barren wasteland.

Cautiously we peer into a blackened crater. Inside, the milky lime-green crater-lake is peacefully sublime in comparison with the highly active vent, which spews forth a constant torrent of burnt-black ash and billowing gaseous vapours.

"It's as though the earth is alive," says Bob, looking around in horror as the ground shakes and a deep rumbling sound comes from beneath our feet.

By the time we return to Whakatane and check into our motel the sun has set. We have takeaways for dinner and with the thunderous roar of the island's gassy belches still ringing in our ears, discuss the powerful forces of nature that we've witnessed.

Bob is absolutely stunned by the experience. "I just can't believe it," he repeats over and over again when I tell him that there's nowhere else in the world where you can experience a live marine volcano at such close proximity. "Can we go again tomorrow?" ■

EAST CAPE

The road around the East Cape, which begins its journey in Opotiki and travels around a seemingly endless necklace of picturesque bays to Gisborne, is a unique, seldom seen part of NZ with its own distinctive style and personality.

If you choose to drive this route don't be surprised if you find horses tied up outside the Four Square store while locals shop inside, or if you're invited to go pig hunting or fishing, or even offered a bed at a local marae.

Opotiki, the gateway to the East Cape, is where most visitors begin their exploration of this relaxed and friendly region. Although the route can be driven in a day, it's worth taking the time to smell the flowers along the way. With blossoming pohutukawa trees lining the coast from top to toe all summer, their tiny red flowers carpeting the sticky tarmac bright red, it's certainly not hard to do!

In Torere a sight seldom seen by city slickers is the Pig Dog Training School. Hunting is a popular regional activity, and hunters travel from far and wide to test their skill in the rugged Raukumara range.

Venture inland on the East Cape and wilderness encounters await. East of Hawai jetboats and whitewater rafts ply the mighty Motu River, while keen fly fishermen stalk the reclusive brown trout lurking in deep pools at every bend. Mountain biking, horse treks and 4WD adventures provide further options to explore these ranges or you can take a guided walk to the peak of sacred Mt Hikurangi.

It's the first point in NZ to see the sun every day –a uniquely spiritual experience which draws upon the lore of the local Maori, Ngati Porou. Visitors can sample macadamia nut products at Pacific Coast Macadamias in Whanarua Bay or delight in the region's large array of gourmet foods including fresh crayfish, truffles, fine olive oils, award-winning cheeses and superbly crafted wines from Gisborne, NZ's Chardonnay Capital!

There are many historical churches to see en route including the Anglican Christ Church in Raukokore, built in 1895 and on a bit of a lean thanks to the Wahine storm of 1968, and St Mary's Church in Tikitiki, one of the most richly decorated Maori churches in NZ. Its stunning interior features carvings, tukutuku panels and stained glass windows recounting the history of the Ngati Porou.

Historical sites also abound. Whangaparaoa is the site where Maori canoes landed in 1350 AD, and Cook's Cove near Tolaga Bay provided a temporary home for the crew of the Endeavour during Captain James Cook's first exploration of the NZ coastline in 1769. Captain Cook made his first landing in Gisborne on 8 October 1769, seeking fresh food and water. Met by local Maori, he misunderstood their traditional welcome and left the bay without provisions. Naturally upset, he called the area Poverty Bay.

But it's Ruatoria that is the true heartland of the East Cape. Relaxed and friendly it's a mellow town where locals are happy to share their unique lifestyle and culture with visitors. The only remnant of Ruatoria's once troubled past is its local iwi station, 98.1 Radio Ngati Porou. It was started to keep communication flowing in the community; today it simply provides entertainment.

While Te Araroa School claims to have the largest pohutukawa tree in NZ (Te Waha o Rerekohu is over 600 years old and has 22 trunks and a girth of 19.9 metres), Gisborne District also holds two world class tree collections at the Eastwoodhill and Hackfalls Arboretums. Plus there are many other town and country gardens for aficionados to explore.
Whangara is the home of *Whale Rider*, and the site where this acclaimed NZ movie was filmed. A plaque on the northern end of Wainui Beach further south marks the spot where 59 sperm whales were buried in 1970 after becoming stranded on the sand.

Gisborne markets itself extensively as the first city to see the sun, but that's not its only attraction. Tairawhiti museum has a fascinating collection of Maori and European artefacts and photos dating back to the 1800s, while at Maia Gallery, a contemporary art studio, students enrolled in Tairawhiti Polytechnic's Toihoukura School of Performing and Visual Arts display their work. ■

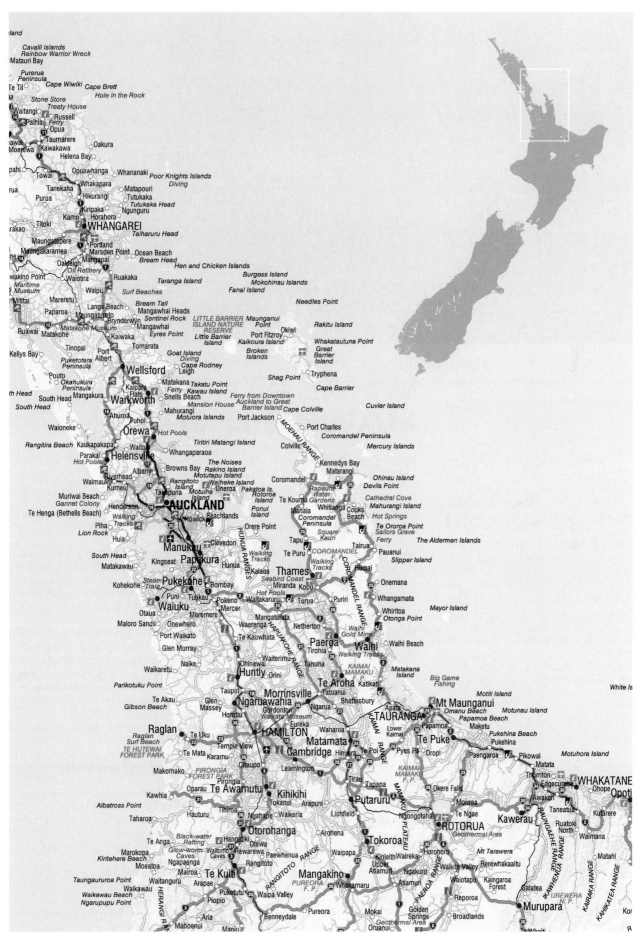

Set amidst jewel-like crater lakes, Rotorua offers stunning, contrasting scenery in an active volcanic wonderland of spouting geysers, bubbling mud pools, fumaroles and natural thermal springs and spas. Further south, NZ's largest lake, Lake Taupo, is fed by sparkling ice-melt from the mountains of the Tongariro National Park. It too was formed by volcanic activity – an eruption so large it was recorded by Chinese and Roman writers. The region's extraordinary landscape and unique range of cultural experiences make it a 'must-see' on any NZ itinerary.

We spend three days travelling from Whakatane to Napier via Rotorua and Taupo. We explore several thermal parks, soak in hot pools, enjoy a traditional Maori hangi, dine on trout, take a balloon ride over the Huka Falls, and travel the historic Taupo-Napier highway to the Art Deco city of Napier and the gannet colony at Cape Kidnappers.

WHAKATANE TO HAWKE'S BAY

DAY ONE
Whakatane to Rotorua

White Island splutters on the horizon as we bid Whakatane farewell and drive inland on SH30 past Mt Edgecumbe's tall cinder cone to Lake Rotoma. It's our first glimpse of the lakes for which Rotorua is renowned.

We stop at Hell's Gate in Tikitere, home to Rotorua's most violent thermal activity, which Bob's keen to see after the excitement of our White Island sojourn. We walk on platforms over a fiery landscape that features not only a mud volcano but also the largest hot water falls in the Southern Hemisphere. Adjacent at the popular Wai Ora Spa we watch women cake themselves with detoxifying mud then soak in warm thermal pools. Bob's tempted but it's a bit early in the day for me.

We drive into Rotorua where we visit more thermal activity at Whakarewarewa and watch spellbound as the famous Pohutu geyser erupts in a spray of boiling water. Whakarewarewa is also home to the Maori Arts and Crafts Institute where we see trainee carvers, weavers and greenstone sculptors using traditional techniques to craft a wide range of wares.

On Lake Rotorua's waterfront we lunch in the company of graceful black swans, then stroll through the Edwardian elegance of the Government Gardens past the world-famous Bath House building, which houses a museum, before turning back to the car.

Rotorua is a whirlwind of activity but the real beauty of the region lies in its natural surroundings and it's easy to find a quiet place away from the crowds.

I take Bob for a drive to Lake Tarawera, stopping briefly at the Blue and Green Lakes to admire their respective colours before continuing on to our destination, which basks under Mt Tarawera's sultry gaze.

So tranquil are the surroundings, it's hard to imagine that this sleeping giant was responsible for one of the worst natural disasters in NZ's history. On the night of June 10th 1886 Mt Tarawera erupted, killing 151 people in the surrounding area and destroying one of Rotorua's popular attractions, the Pink and White Terraces.

At the Buried Village, you can relive the terror of the eruption and tour the excavated remains of Te Wairoa, a village buried in rocks, ash and boiling hot mud.

Back in Rotorua we check into our accommodation and our kind host books us in for a traditional hangi at the Tamaki Maori Village. There are more than two hours before our pickup by coach, so we cross the road to the Polynesian Spa.

It caters for everyone with family pools, adult only pools, and private pools as well as the stunningly peaceful lake spa retreat. While Bob relaxes in the soft alkaline waters of a shallow rock pool overlooking the lake, I book myself in for an Aix massage followed by a

refreshing lavender and honey body polish. Feeling like a new person I rejoin Bob and we spend a blissfully quiet time watching the sun sinking over Mokoia Island, the setting for one of the greatest Maori love stories ever told.

Rotorua is rich with Maori folklore and legend and there's no better way to gain a greater insight than to visit the Tamaki Maori village at Te Tawa Ngahere Pa. Here we experience Maori culture first hand with a traditional powhiri (welcome ceremony) before taking a journey back through time, experiencing the pre-European lifestyle and customs of the Maori through tribal songs, dances and activities. After an uplifting kapa haka (song and dance) performance, we all share in a traditional hangi meal, cooked on hot stones underground. It's delicious and Bob, who had earlier expressed some reservations about "earthy food", pronounces it divine and spends the evening debating the merits of earth ovens with Maori elders.

DAY TWO
Rotorua to Taupo

We welcome a slower start to the day but I hurry Bob along somewhat as I have a special treat in store.

At 10 am we pull into the carpark at Wai-O-Tapu, purchase tickets and join a small group seated at the Lady Knox geyser. "It only erupts once a day," I say. We sit down to wait and after five minutes Bob's beginning to fidget. After ten he strums his fingers on his knees. Finally he says: "We could be waiting all day."

At 10.15 sharp a park ranger walks to the geyser and begins to tell her story. The Lady Knox was accidentally discovered in 1896 when prisoners washing their laundry were interrupted by a towering spray of water out of the ground. Now, every day at 10.15, the geyser is coaxed into action with Sunlight soap, much to the amazement of onlookers - including Bob, who waggles his finger at me as the hot soapy water spouts high.

After that, we take a walk through the park's panoramic hot and cold pools, fumaroles and boiling mud, which display an amazing array of colours. For a time we sit beside the bubbling champagne pool with its impressive ochre-tinged edge.

Then we continue to Taupo and stop at Prawn Farm in Wairakei Tourist Park, a geothermal-heated prawn farm where kiwi ingenuity is at its finest! Fresh water tropical prawns flourish here in recycled geothermal water from Wairakei Power Station. We take a short tour, then dine on freshly harvested prawns at its restaurant overlooking the Waikato River. NZ's longest river, it begins its 425 kilometre journey to the sea from Lake Taupo where it pushes through a long narrow gorge before plunging over the Huka Falls. There are a number of good walks in the area but instead we opt for a balloon ride with Peter Paalvast, or Captain Pierre as he's known around town.

Joining a couple of other aspiring aviators we climb into the basket - which proves to be a bit of a palaver for Bob after one too many prawns. Captain Pierre fires up the gas and off we gently float, climbing higher and higher above Huka Falls and descending so we hover just over the tumultuous ice-blue cascade. Bob's face turns blue from the reflection – or perhaps he's holding his breath – and then we drift upwards, skimming the tops of tall

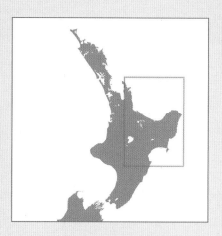

Whakatane to Hawke's Bay:
Attractions and Activities

Hells Gate: www.hellsgate.co.nz

Agrodome: www.agrodome.co.nz

Whakarewarewa: www.whakarewarewa.com

The Buried Village: www.buriedvillage.co.nz

Polynesian Spa: www.polynesianspa.co.nz

Tamaki Maori Village: www.maoriculture.co.nz

Wai-O-Tapu: www.geyserland.co.nz

Absolutely Angling: www.wilderness.co.nz

Art Deco Walk: www.artdeconapier.com

Gannet Beach Adventures: www.gannets.com

Whakatane to Hawke's Bay:
Cafés and Eateries

Tamaki Village Hangi: SH5, Rotorua

Pig and Whistle: 1182 Tutanekai St, Rotorua

Capers Epicurean: 1181 Eruera St, Rotorua

Prawn Farm: SH5, Taupo

Replete Food Company: 45 Heu Heu St, Taupo

De Luca's Café: Emerson Street, Napier

The Thirsty Whale: 62 West Quay, Napier

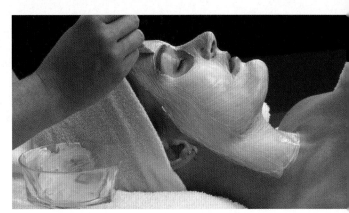

> We watch ladies cake themselves with detoxifying mud then soak in warm thermal pools

trees before landing with a bump by the lake. Here, as is the ballooning custom (and not a bad one at that!), our safe landing is celebrated with a bottle of champagne.

After collecting our car we visit the Taupo information centre which provides an exhaustive list of things to do: cruising on the lake to Maori rock carvings; taking a spin in a jet boat; parachuting; paraponting; playing golf; kayaking; sailing; windsurfing; fly fishing; bungy jumping; hiking and so the list goes on.

With so much on offer it almost seems sinful to relax, but relax we do, after first checking into our beachfront accommodation. Bob drags two deck chairs down onto Lake Taupo's crisp pumice sands and here, against a stunning backdrop of snowy capped mountains in the Tongariro National Park, we watch everyone else's energetic antics.

Late in the day dinner comes courtesy of our hosts Tim and Jan, who on the spur of the moment decide to "throw the line in" from their runabout. Spotting us on the lakeshore they ask if we'd like to come along for the ride. Bob's on board in a jiffy, getting soaked in the process such is his haste. I climb onboard too: rainbow and

brown trout thrive in these parts and you'd be mad not to try your hand angling if given half a chance.

The boys throw the lines in and before long Bob's rod bends tautly and the reel spins – it's a strike! A beautiful rainbow trout leaps out of the water, bucking furiously. It puts on a good show, writhing two or three times before it tires and Bob gleefully pulls it aboard in the net.

"She's a beauty," says Tim, "A good seven pounds at least." It's a good fish alright, thick through the middle with a glossy coat. Bob's delighted and after a quick grin at the camera, he carefully extracts the hook and slings his line back into the lake. "If I could catch trout like this at home I'd be a happy man," he says.

Back on terra firma Tim carries the catch to a filleting table on the lake edge and we watch as he skilfully guts the fish. Its flesh is pink with an almost orange hue. Tim says this is unique to Lake Taupo as the fish feed on koura (native crayfish) which gives their flesh an apricot tone and an extra yummy almost salmon-like flavour.

While the trout smokes we enjoy a glass of wine or two (courtesy of Bob's West Auckland wine-spending spree) and exchange fishy tales, then enjoy a meal of delectable smoked trout with fresh salad greens.

DAY THREE
Taupo to Napier

After a leisurely breakfast and a stroll along the lakeshore we set off bound for Napier on SH5, following a route forged in 1874 when a two-day Taupo-Napier Highway coach service began.

These days it takes around two hours. We make a stop at Waipunga Falls where there's a parking area and viewing point. Bob takes a photo and then we continue to Tarawera which provided a resting point overnight for passengers taking the Taupo-Napier coach service. Comfort for the travellers included a soak in the hot sodium springs on the banks of the Waipunga River.

Before long we hit the orchards and vineyards of the Esk Valley

where citrus fruit, avocados and grapes are grown, indicating that we've arrived in Hawke's Bay. When we enter Napier itself, Bob is struck by the wealth of art deco and Spanish Mission style buildings. I relay the story of the 1931 earthquake and the subsequent rebuilding of the town in the modern architecture of the time.

We join an informative one-hour walking tour of the inner city's buildings with Doreen Smith, a knowledgeable volunteer guide for the Art Deco Trust. Bob's already pretty good at spotting the zigzags, sunbursts and fountain shapes that characterise the design of the period, but soon I'm like a professional too. Seeing how keen Bob is, Doreen recommends we return for one of the Art Deco Weekends held in February and July. It's a time when folk polish their vintage cars, dress in their best art deco gear and take part in 'bubbly' breakfasts, café crawls, celebrity tea parties, and glitzy costume and coiffure competitions. Doreen's already got a gorgeous frilly black skirt and black feather band lined up for the next event! After a lunch of freshly made bagels at De Luca's Café, we finish the day with a tractor and trailer ride out to the gannet colony

at Cape Kidnappers. This is a nostalgic trip for me and although Bob's not so keen "to take a bumpy beach ride" he soon gets into the spirit of things as our tractor and trailer set off in a convoy with two others along the beach.

Access to this unique gannet colony is only available at low tide and we pass massive white sandstone cliffs en route. Our driver points out fragmented fault and tilt lines along the way which tell the story of the region's many earthquakes.

We stop near the cape and walk uphill to where gannets – in their thousands – nest on a rocky plateau. An hour and a half is given to spend time viewing the birds before we board our trailer and journey back along the beach. On the return I share my vivid memories of this trip as a child with Bob as we bounce back towards Napier. The dolphins at Marineland were another highlight that I remember clearly and I wonder out loud if we should visit tomorrow. "Perhaps," says Bob distractedly as his tummy gives a distinctly loud growl, "but more importantly can you remember where you ate dinner?" ■

ROTORUA ACTION

As well as cultural attractions and activities, Rotorua is a hot spot for adventurous - if not downright wacky - entertainment. From having a ball in a Zorb to flying with Freefall Xtreme there are any number of ways to indulge in extreme sports. The bulk of these activities can be found at the Agrodome in Ngongotaha, a small lakeside settlement six kilometres from the city centre.

The Zorb is a simple concept: a big, fat, clear plastic ball into which you climb before being rolled down a hill. You're protected from serious harm by an air cushion between you and the ground, but if this is too tame you can always add another person, or throw in a bucket of water!

Then there's Freefall Extreme: kitted up in a flying suit, goggles and gloves, you wait spread-eagled belly-down on a black net twenty metres above a 900 hp twin turbo V12 diesel powered DC3 aircraft propeller ready for takeoff. When the engine revs a blast of air travelling at over 150 kph hits your body and it's like being blown to pieces by a giant hairdryer – without the heat. Your hair flaps, skin stretches tautly, ears pin themselves back in the whipping wind and suddenly you begin to levitate, rising slowly like a helicopter, hovering higher and higher until you're two metres above the net and held aloft by the rushing jet stream. It's a sensationally exhilarating experience but staying airborne is a lot harder than it looks. It takes a lot of practice before you can swoop and soar like a pro.

Instructors recommend pushing out your chest and using your arms like rudders but if all else fails a soft 12-metre wide giant air cushion surrounding the netting makes for a soft landing. But it should come with a warning: defying gravity like this is highly addictive!

The Agrodome provides a wide range of other adrenaline-pumping activities to choose from: you can bungy jump from a 43-metre tower over the Ngongotaha River; take a 40-metre high swing with friends on the giant Swoop reaching speeds of up to 130 kph and a G-force factor of three; or take a thrilling jetsprint ride on the Hydrojet, a 450 hp jet propelled raceboat that gets you up to 100 kph in 4.5 seconds on a water course laid out like a race track. It's an exhilarating ride that is sure to leave you feeling weak at the knees.

If your adrenal gland still begs for more, head to Off-Road NZ in Mamaku, just north of Rotorua. Here you can put your four wheel driving skills to the test on their bush safari which travels along steep, rough tracks, through muddy waterholes and tunnels, and across precariously positioned bridges to the luge, a steep seven metre slope requiring a controlled skid into knee deep water. There's also a sprint car track or you can take a spin in the monster 4x4.

For those with more mainstream tastes, Helipro offers scenic flights over Rotorua, or you can try any number of other popular outdoor activities including mountain biking, white water rafting and kayaking.

At the Whakarewarewa Forest, there's an extensive network of mountain biking trails to suit all levels of ability. Planet Bike provides bike and equipment hire, instruction for beginners through to advanced and a variety of all-inclusive mountain biking tours through the forest. For a novice the two hour first-timers special is a good deal. You can learn the basics such as braking and gear changing, downhill and uphill positioning and how to ride through mud, sand and gravel.

Whitewater rafting action can be found at Lake Rotoiti, where the highest commercially rafted waterfall in the world waits to be conquered. Standing seven metres high and rated grade five (grade six is not commercially raftable in New Zealand), it's the ultimate adrenaline rush.

You can also tandem kayak over the same falls with Kenny Mutton - NZ's very own World Freestyle Bronze Medallist - who has kayaked the Kaituna River "on and off for ten years." Ken offers expert tuition for beginners through to advanced, and after a three hour lesson he says most people have the skills to take on the waterfall all by themselves! ■

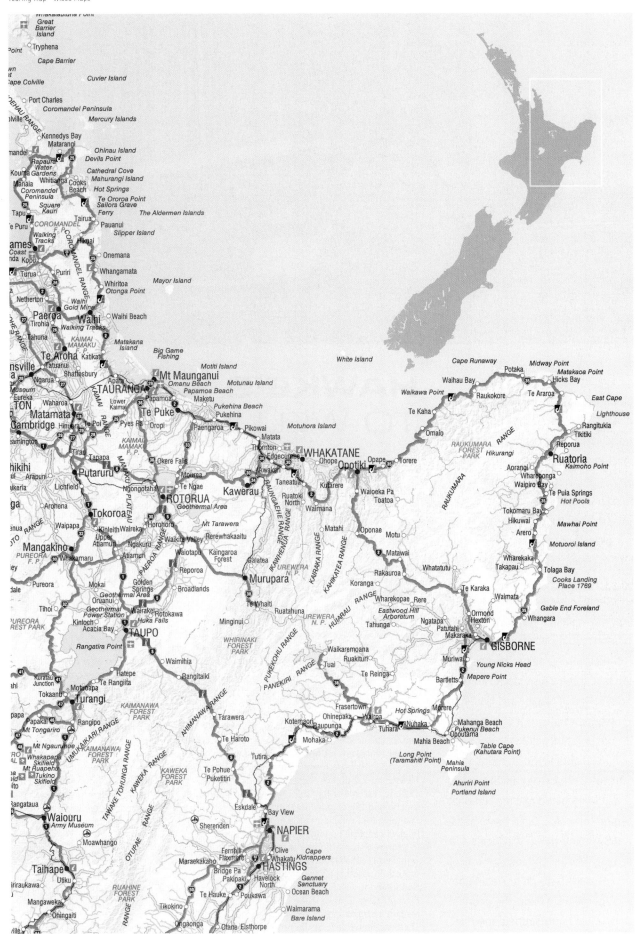

Located on the east coast of the North Island, Hawke's Bay is one of NZ's premier food, wine and lifestyle destinations. Home to NZ's oldest operational winery it's also the largest red wine producing region in the country. Wine lovers will discover more than 50 wineries in the region; over 30 of them provide a cellar door experience where you can visit, tour and taste. At some of the more boutique style vineyards such as Clearview Estate the knowledgeable person actually pouring the wine is often the winemaker themselves! We take three days to tour Hawke's Bay towns of Napier and Hastings where we fill our picnic hamper to bursting point with gourmet delights found en route, then travel south to the capital city. We visit Marineland and the National Aquarium of NZ, taste the regions' award winning wines, join locals at a Farmers' Market and follow a trail of museums south to Wellington, home of Te Papa, the greatest museum of them all.

HAWKE'S BAY TO WELLINGTON

DAY ONE
Napier

Marineland is at the top of our list of activities. Why? Because I've discovered that the dolphins I watched in awe at eight years of age are the very same ladies performing today!

Bob and I join the 9.30 am 'Touch and Feed' and Marineland's Education Officer, Bridey White, takes us behind the scenes. Bob and Bridey hit it off immediately and we discover that she began work here as a twelve-year-old volunteer. Quarter of a century later, she still shares an intimate relationship with her old friends, Kelly and Shona.

"They're the oldest common dolphins in the world to be housed in a marine park," says Bridey. "Most common dolphins live to around 15 to 18 years of age so they're doing well in their mid-thirties."

We make our way over to their pool where the dolphins appear in fine fettle and consume our fishy gifts with gusto.

Seated on a grandstand we watch them play ball just as I did once as a little girl many moons ago, then take a walk around the centre which is home to injured creatures, from sea lions through to sea gulls. Those who recover adequately are released back into the wild while others, like little Onion, a blue penguin who has constant inner ear infections, become permanent residents.

After a relaxing lunch at a café on Napier's Marine Parade we view Hawke's Bay Museum and Exhibition Centre. There are extensive exhibits of contemporary and traditional Maori art, ceramics, textiles and the social history of the region, but we agree that the highlight is Survivors' Stories, a riveting video telling the tale of Napier's devastating 1931 earthquake.

Measuring 7.9 on the Richter Scale, the quake hit the city at 10.46 am on 3rd February, 1931. In two-and-a-half minutes, Napier and nearby Hastings were literally shaken to the ground and 258 people lost their lives in what remains NZ's worst natural disaster.

The town was rebuilt and the former ornate Victorian architecture replaced with the clean lines of concrete buildings of art deco design.

In search of some lighter entertainment we continue with our morning's aquatic theme with a visit to the National Aquarium of NZ. It's home to a wide range of NZ marine animals and other native species, including the tuatara and kiwi.

Bob's keen to watch the feeding show and so we hop aboard the travelator, which journeys through glass tunnels in the oceanarium, where, much to our delight, we see a diver hand-feeding a large stingray and shark.

Then we spend time at the not-so-native Possum World, where the skins of these pesky creatures are used to create beautifully styled blankets, slippers and hats. A local busi-

ness, it relies on possums caught in nearby forests, and after the skins are dressed, they're sponged, stretched, stencilled and sewn on site. There's a small museum to look around; it's free, and features fun, educational displays on NZ's possum plague. Bob picks up a gorgeous blanket, "Could come in handy in the South Island," he jokes, packing it away in the boot.

We end the day at the Ocean Spa on Marine Parade in new open-air heated pools built on the site of Napier's original Hot Sea Water Baths. There are various leisure pools as well as a 25-metre lap pool. Bob does a couple of laps and then breathlessly gives up and joins me in an elevated adult-only spa where we relax and watch the sunset cast a pinkish light on the white cliffs of Cape Kidnappers.

DAY TWO
Napier to Hastings

After a continental breakfast inhouse, Bob's keen to depart early. Today's plan is to visit several vineyards and sample gourmet products created in specialist kitchens in the region.

But first we drive to the richly ornate art deco National Tobacco Company building in Ahuriri, then through the art deco suburb of Marewa to Taradale's McDeco McDee's. It was formerly the Taradale Hotel, but in 1997 it was converted into a McDonalds.

But a burger is out of the question as Taradale is also home to some of Hawke's Bay's finest vineyards. We visit Mission Estate, NZ's oldest winery, established in 1851 by the Marist Brothers. Its tasting room, cellar, restaurant and gallery are all housed inside a former seminary building nestled high on a plateau and it has a special ambience. We enjoy a small tasting then wash it down with a latté on a verandah overlooking the vines.

The next stop is at Taradale's 114 Avocados where we have a complimentary tasting. I purchase ten avocados in various stages of ripeness for our picnic basket while Bob collects recipes from the owner, and then it's on to Ruby Glen where we wander amongst the brambles collecting our own raspberries. Bob ends up looking like he's wearing lipstick – more berries end up in his mouth than the collection basket – and his face turns the same colour when the checkout operator laughs and says his mouth is 'Ruby Red', like most who visit here.

Before hitting Hastings, we drive out to the coast at Te Awanga for lunch at Clearview Estate. When we arrive, winemaker Tim Turvey leaves the shed where he's busy testing barrels and walks over to greet us. He leads us to an atmospheric tasting room, where riddling racks line the walls and cobbled floors meet tables crafted from wine barrels.

We're guided through the vineyard's range of organic wine, and then we have our lunch at an informal dining table and chairs built around an 80-year-old olive tree. I try the panfried snapper while Bob tucks into a brioche and anchovy-crusted lamb rack; they're both delicious!

After lunch we visit Goodin Grove where we taste a variety of organic extra virgin olive oils and collect a bottle for the picnic basket before driving to the Silky Oak Chocolate Company. As we step inside the smell of rich cocoa nearly bowls us over. "Wow," says Bob, "I think we've arrived in heaven!"

Through the glass partitions we watch as workers craft the chocolate. A video plays in the corner and explains that only 100 per cent pure cocoa butter is used, but we've no time

Hawke's Bay to Wellington:
Attractions and Activities

Marineland: www.marineland.co.nz

Hawke's Bay Museum: www.hawkesbaymuseum.co.nz

National Aquarium: www.nationalaquarium.co.nz

Possum World: Marine Parade, Napier

Ocean Spa: www.findus.co.nz/oceanspa

Silky Oak Chocolate Co: www.silkyoakchocs.co.nz

The Rugby Museum: www.rugbymuseum.co.nz

Mt Bruce Wildlife Centre: www.mtbruce.org.nz

Fell Engine Museum: Featherston

Te Papa: www.tepapa.govt.nz

Hawke's Bay to Wellington:
Cafés and Eateries

Mission Estate Winery: Church Rd, Taradale

Clearview Estate Winery: Clifton Rd, RD2, Hastings

Sileni Estate Winery: 2016 Maraekakaho Rd, Hastings

Hawthorne Coffee Roastery: 23 Napier Rd, Havelock Nth

Craggy Range: 253 Waimarama Rd, Havelock Nth

Sunday Farmers' Market: Hawke's Bay Showgrounds

Lady Featherston Café: 31 Fitzherbert St, Featherston

Te Mata Peak, Havelock North - Donna Blaber
below: Te Papa at dusk - Positively Wellington Tourism

Marineland Napier - Donna Blaber
below: Relaxing in Wine Country - Hawkes Bay Tourism

> I purchase ten avocados in various stages of ripeness for our picnic basket while Bob collects recipes from the owner

for that – we're here to savour their wares. The cabinet displays a seemingly endless selection of chocolate from truffles to liqueurs, crèmes to caramels and even a chilli-chocolate blend!

In the midst of a chocoholic frenzy triggered by the intense aromas, it's too hard to make a selection, so in the end, Bob says "what the heck," and we simply take two of each. That sorted, we leave with our embarrassingly extra-large paper bag and proceed to sample chocolates all the way to Sileni Estate. It's long, sweeping driveway and symmetrical architecture is designed to impress so we carefully check for telltale chocolate smears on our faces before stepping out to taste some of the classic wine varieties on offer.

But fine wine was only one of the elements that attracted us here: Sileni also has a well stocked pantry which provides a roundup of all that's on offer in Hawke's Bay and a temperature-controlled room that provides the perfect setting for cheese to ripen. There's a culinary school onsite and after perusing the list of courses Bob discusses returning for a class after we've completed our circumnavigation of NZ.

As Bob considers the pros and cons we drive to Havelock North to immerse ourselves in the aromas, tastes and sounds of the Hawthorne Coffee Roastery and Espresso Bar.

Next stop is Craggy Range vineyard nestled beneath Te Mata Peak, and then we drive to the top for breathtaking views of the surrounding countryside. The peak is known to the Maori as Te Mata o Rongokako (the face of Rongokako) and according to legend, Rongokako was challenged to eat his way through the peak to win the hand of the beautiful Muriwhenua. He choked on a rock and fell to the ground.

Bob can relate to the challenge. "I feel like I've eaten a track through Napier and Hastings," he says, pointing below to where lights are beginning to come on one by one, "Look you can see where we've been!" A strong wind blows and grey clouds stack up on the horizon as we retreat to the warmth and comfort of a country B&B just south of Hastings. Our hosts provide a delicious dinner of roast beef followed by generous helpings of chocolate berry roulade, and we fall asleep to the patter of rain.

DAY THREE
Hastings to Wellington

In the morning the sun is shining again. We skip breakfast and head into Hastings for the Sunday Farmers' Market at Hawke's Bay Showgrounds. Here we enjoy hot bacon and egg rolls washed down with freshly roasted coffee before we shop in the old-fashioned way, meeting the growers and producers and chatting about their products. From handmade cheeses, to bread, icecream, chocolates (again!), meat and seasonal fruits and vegetables, there's plenty on offer.

We buy cheese and a selection of breads to join the raspberries and avocados already in our picnic basket. "We'll have a health day today," announces Bob, averting his gaze as we pass the chocolate stand en route to the car.

We leave town and drive south on SH2 through Waipukurau, Dan-

nevirke and Woodville where a side trip on SH3 leads through Manawatu Gorge Scenic Reserve. Here we enjoy a picnic from our basket on tables overlooking the river before continuing to Palmerston North, where The Rugby Museum has a comprehensive collection of rugby memorabilia and reflects the passion New Zealander's have for the game.

Back on SH2 we head south to the Mt Bruce Wildlife Centre some 28 kilometres north of Masterton. It was started to breed the takahe after its rediscovery in 1948 and is home to many other endangered native birds such as black stilts, North Island kokako, saddleback and kiwis. However it's the colourful takahe that we're here to see and so we watch a breeding pair in an adjoining enclosure while enjoying a pot of tea.

Then its on to Masterton, the so-called heart of the Wairarapa with its early childhood museum, to Greytown, where Victorian buildings line the main street of NZ's first planned inland town, established in 1853. As we pass the Cobblestone and the Toy Soldier Museum Bob comments that it's somewhat of a trend in these parts.

"We're following a museum trail that leads to the mother of them all in Wellington," he says, referring to Te Papa.

In Featherston we discover two further unique museums: the Fell Engine Museum which houses the only fell engine in the world and the Featherston Heritage Museum which commemorates the Featherston military camp from WWI and its role as a Japanese prisoner of war camp in WWII.

We're tempted to stop but Te Papa's pull is too strong. We drive over the windy, bush covered Rimutaka Ranges and through Upper and Lower Hutt before arriving in the capital city.

Te Papa, NZ's National Museum, stands proudly on Wellington's waterfront.

"Good," says Bob checking his watch at the entrance, "there's a couple of hours 'til closing."

Within moments of our arrival we are lost in the taonga (Maori cultural treasures), history and stories of NZ. There are five floors spread over the equivalent of three rugby fields and we're halfway through the photo gallery when a curator approaches.

"It's riveting," Bob tells the man.

"Indeed it is," says the curator with a smile, "but we actually closed half an hour ago."

Bob forlornly checks his watch.

"We open again at 10 o'clock tomorrow," says the curator helpfully, "You're welcome to return."

"Oh we will," says Bob reverently as he turns to me, "let's schedule it in." ■

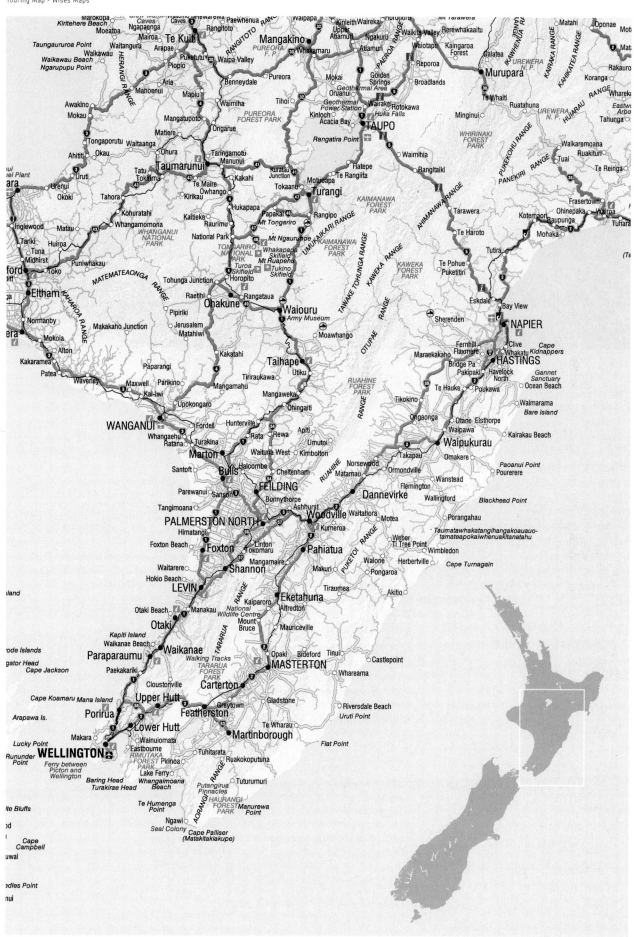

The scenery of the southern Wairarapa is ruggedly dramatic: rolling tablelands end abruptly and form high textured cliffs which plummet to meet the seaweed and driftwood-strewn coastline; the Rimutaka Ranges cast shadows over the shimmering expanse of Lake Wairarapa; and to the north the Tararua Ranges tower over fertile plains. At the centre of all this wonderful scenery is Martinborough, a town dubbed NZ's pinot noir capital and one that is well known not only for its quality wines, but also for its top winemakers who have earned international recognition for their award-winning pinot noir and sauvignon blanc.

We take two days to explore the region and visit Cape Palliser lighthouse, meet seals on the beach, dine on crayfish and delicious green-lipped mussels, call into the cellars of several of Martinborough's top vineyards, follow the local arts trail and take an unforgettable quad bike ride on Lachie McLeod's farm.

WAIRARAPA

DAY ONE
Wellington to Martinborough
with a side trip to Cape Palliser

We leave Wellington in the early morning and reach Featherston, the gateway to the Wairarapa, by 9.30 am. Breakfast – stacks of Vogel's toast washed down with copious cups of tea – is enjoyed in a good old fashioned kiwi tearoom on the main street. "Have you seen the Fell engine?" enquires our waitress when she delivers a fresh pot of steaming tea to our table, "It's the only one left in the world."

We decide to stretch our legs around the museum after breakfast and discover that it houses not only the fell engine, the sole survivor of the rolling stock of the Rimutaka Incline, but also an incline brake van and many other items of railroad memorabilia.

From Featherston we head south, skimming the shores of Lake Wairarapa - the largest wetlands in the lower North Island and home to both native and migratory birds - before crossing the Ruamahanga River to Lake Ferry.

This small settlement has views overlooking the pounding waves of Palliser Bay and across the tranquil waters of Lake Onoke. The lake is fed with fresh water from the Ruamahanga River and is sheltered from the ocean by a narrow sandy spit. Bob and I kick off our shoes and walk the length of the spit - the contrast between the two is quite astounding.

Before we leave town Bob, ever mindful of his stomach, makes a note that the hotel serves steamed green-lipped mussels, "Let's come back for lunch," he says.

We drive slightly inland before meeting the coast again at the Putangirua Pinnacles, where we hike upstream to these huge, organ pipe-like columns which were formed over the past 120,000 years by heavy rain washing away silt and sand to expose the underlying bedrock. Bob takes several photos and on the return we notice that there's also a small amount of erosion on the rocks above the car park – they provide an ideal glimpse for visitors who are unable to hike in to see the pinnacles.

In Ngawi, a picturesque fishing village located at the base of the towering Aorangi Range, we're greeted by rows of rusty, brightly-painted bulldozers parked on the beach. We watch the fishermen as they haul sturdy fishing boats ashore using the bulldozers and then stack crayfish pots in neat piles around the village.

"The seafood looks promising," remarks Bob, as we pass wooden houses surrounded by wire fences which are draped with strings of faded buoys.

Shortly before Cape Palliser Lighthouse Bob spots some seals lazing on the rocky shore and we stop to admire these beautiful beasts, making certain that we keep the recommended ten metre gap between us and them.

"They're a lot bigger than I'd imagined," says Bob, cautiously pulling out his camera as a seal raises his head and warily opens one eye to see who his visitors are.

Above the beach, high on the edge of a weather beaten cliff, the lighthouse stands sentry.

It was constructed in 1896 from materials brought here by boat, as there was no road for many years.

We hike the 258 extremely steep steps to the top from where, at the southern most point of the North Island, we gain magnificent views across the wide boiling expanse of Cook Strait to the snowcapped mountains of Kaikoura. Thunderous surf crashes onto the rocks below and sends sheets of salt-laden spray flying. As we gaze across the windswept horseshoe of Palliser Bay, it's hard to believe that these shores provided the principle point of access for early European settlers to the region.

"It's rugged but breathtaking," says Bob, as we watch the spaghetti-like kelp weave a never-ending pattern.

We return along the coast enjoying reverse views of the picturesque coastline and stop in for a late lunch at the hotel in Lake Ferry. Bob chooses the crayfish while I have the deliciously fresh, steamed green-lipped mussels before we drive inland to Martinborough, a peaceful town where life revolves around a leafy town square. There are many notable buildings built around the square which have been restored to their former glory, including the landmark Martinborough Hotel. We check into stylish rooms and then head across the road to the Martinborough Wine Centre, a good first stop in this town for those planning to discover local wines. Here we learn that the district's dry alluvial river terraces provide ideal conditions for growing healthy vines. This combined with low rainfall and a temperate climate - hot summer days and reliable dry autumns - encourages winemakers to hang their grapes later and results in a more intense flavour with no obvious loss in acidity.

We sample wine styles from a variety of local vineyards, choose our favourites, then head out to explore - armed with a copy of the Martinborough wine trail map.

Our journey begins at Te Kairanga vineyard. The site upon which this vineyard stands was the first place in Martinborough to be planted in vines. The cellar door is positioned in sheltered gardens and here we meet Catherine Hannagan, who guides us through our tasting. A local through and through she tells us that she was in Martinborough before the vineyards started. Impressed with their Pinot Noir - not to mention Catherine's friendly manner - Bob purchases a couple of bottles.

Then we call into Ata Rangi and Chifney vineyards where we enjoy a tasting, and on to Martinborough Vineyard where we strike it lucky and delight in a relaxed conversation with winemaker, Claire Mulholland. She tells us that she has spent several vintages overseas – three in France, two harvests in the US and one in Australia. "You learn something from every harvest," she says, going on to explain how vine age influences the depth of structure in wine. "Our vineyards in NZ are still very young compared to anything in Europe," she says.

We pass Benfield and Delamare where workers are busy 'tucking in' the vines and then at Winslow we strike a rapport with Jenny, who, as well as producing wine with her husband Steve, works as an artist and is well known for her mixed media masks. 'Petra', a stunning mask on the wall behind the tasting bar features on their Cabernet label. "Steve and I bought the property 20 years ago," she says, "Three paddocks and a couple of cows. It's been a lot of work. Our wines must be exceptional to compete with the big wine makers."

But as Bob notes from reading a brochure, even Martinborough's largest producer, Palliser Estate, began production on a small scale and grew as demand increased, today exporting

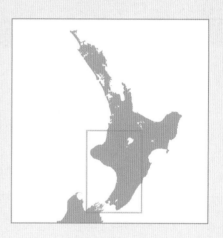

Wairarapa:
Attractions and Activities

Fell Engine Museum: Featherston
Palliser Lighthouse: Cape Palliser
Martinborough Wine Centre: www.martinboroughwinecentre.co.nz
Te Kairanga Vineyard: www.tekairanga.co.nz
Ata Rangi: www.atarangi.co.nz
Martinborough Vineyard: www.martinborough-vineyard.co.nz
Benfield & Delamare: www.benfieldanddelamare.co.nz
Winslow Wines: www.winslowwines.co.nz
McLeods Quad Adventures: www.mcleods-martinborough.co.nz
Jet Boating: www.adventurejet.co.nz

Wairarapa:
Cafés and Eateries

Nesmody Café: 76 Fitzherbert St, Featherston
Lake Ferry Hotel: Lake Ferry, RD2, Featherston
Martinborough Hotel Bistro: The Square, Martinborough
Flying Fish: The Square, Martinborough
The Vines on the Square: The Square, Martinborough
La Mousse: The Square, Martinborough
Riverview Café: Murdoch James Estate,
Dry River Rd, Martinborough

> "The plains of Martinborough's wine country spread below us framed by the sweeping curve of Palliser Bay, the rugged ridgeline of the Rimutakas and the towering Tararua Ranges"

their wine around the world.

Our wine-tasting tour complete for the day – thank goodness, because as the driver I'm thoroughly tired of tasting and spitting and I feel like I've earned a glass of wine – we head to The Martinborough Hotel's corner Settlers Bar for a pre-dinner drink. Locals have told us that this is the place to rub shoulders with well known winemakers. Instead we meet a happy-go-lucky group of mud-splattered Wellingtonians who have apparently just returned from quad biking at McLeod's Farm. "Haven't you heard about Lachie's?" they ask when we enquire, "It's the best ride in town by far!"

Over a light supper of seafood chowder – fresh fish, mussels, prawns, calamari and summer vegetables bound in a light veloute – in the hotel's stylish Bistro we decide that quad biking at Lachie McLeod's farm is simply a must-do.

I'm keen to see the magical views described by the group, while Bob, who learnt to ride a quad bike on our West Auckland sojourn, wants to put his new skills to the test, and so we make a double booking for the next afternoon before retiring to our rooms.

DAY TWO
Martinborough

After breakfasting on crumpets inhouse we decide to spend the morning discovering Martinborough's boutique stores and arts. We begin with a visit to Artrageous, which has displays of contemporary NZ art and sculpture by local and national artists. Here we admire Scott Tulloch's wildlife studies and landscapes, but it's his cartoon series "A Vineyard Year at the Frolicking Pig Estate" that tickles Bob's fancy and before we leave he purchases a print of a hilarious looking pig pushing a wheelbarrow.

Then we pop into the Barbara A. Ross Studio which specialises in traditional Maori weaving and displays a range of textile art, before calling into Barrows Gallery where there's further contemporary NZ artworks on display.

A quick visit to the information centre proves there's no shortage of fun in Martinborough. You can take a spin in a jet boat up the mighty Ruamahanga River with WetnWild, kayak, trek with llamas (if you have a few days up your sleeve), and play golf or golf cross – a revolutionary new game similar to golf but played with an oval ball and goal posts rather than holes to score in!

But for Bob and me, like many other holiday makers, the perfect vacation activity involves the simple act of teaming a good bottle of vino with gourmet food – and in Martinborough it's unlikely that you will be disappointed. The town boasts a number of fine cafes and restaurants, among them the Flying Fish Café, The Vines on the Square and La Mousse, but if you wish to dine in a vineyard setting there is only one place to go and that's to Riverview Café at Murdoch James Estate. It's situated on an elevated slope overlooking Martinborough township, the Dry River, and the Tararua and Rimutaka Ranges. It's a family operation, owned and operated by Jill and Roger Fraser and their son, Carl.

"When we saw the property we realised that we wanted to do more than just have a vineyard," says Roger when Bob and I turn up for an early lunch.

We sit on a terrace table watching children splash in the sparkling river below. The menu is extensive but centres around fresh seasonal local fare which is organic whenever possible. I try the spinach and goats cheese ravioli with a walnut beurre noir, while Bob goes for the cold smoked salmon with pink grapefruit salad and mandarin yoghurt. Both dishes are divine and the setting is so relaxing we'd be happy to stay all day.

But quad biking calls so we take our leave and drive the short distance to McLeod's Quad Adventures. Here we're provided with a helmet, leggings and gumboots and Bob gets me to take several shots of his pristine outfit before we start.

After the training and confidence building course (where Bob gets to show off all he learned in West Auckland) we leave in a convoy, following Lachie out across his massive sheep station on the slopes of the Nga-waka-akupe hills. Up hill and down dale we race, our skills increasing with each new manoeuvre. We splash up the rocky Ruakokopatuna River and cross several other clear streams and deep muddy holes before we climb to the summit of the Nga-waka-akupe. The views are fantastic: the plains of Martinborough's wine country are spread immediately below us framed by the sweeping curve of Palliser Bay, the rugged ridgeline of the Rimutakas and the towering Tararua Ranges.

"It's a grand view," Bob says to Lachie who stands with his hands on his hips smiling at our group of muddy quad bikers who peer through their camera lenses trying to get the whole view in one shot.

"How'd you hear 'bout us?" he asks Bob, grinning.

"Oh you know," says Bob about to wipe a dirty smudge from his face then quite clearly deciding against it. "Through the grapevine..." ■

Bay of Islands - Deerace Publishing

TAKE THE SCENIC ROUTE WITH APEX

100% NEW ZEALAND CAR HIRE

WWW.APEXRENTALS.COM

Fifty minutes drive north of Wellington, the Kapiti Coast is well known for its exceptional cheese and unique flora and fauna. Many of NZ's most endangered birds reside on this coastline which leads north to Wanganui, a historic riverboat town. It once formed part of a thriving tourist route between Auckland and Wellington, and today this bygone era is recreated aboard NZ's only coal-fired paddle steamer, the *PS Waimarie*. Further north the symmetrical volcanic cone of Mt Taranaki can be seen clearly on the horizon. Taranaki's bulbous coastline is tucked firmly around two-thirds of this zen-like mountain, providing NZ's most consistent surf conditions. Access is provided courtesy of SH45, the Surf Highway, which follows around the coast from Hawera to New Plymouth.

We spend three days exploring the coast from Wellington to New Plymouth. Bob milks his first cow and I take a tandem surf ride. Together we sample Kapiti's award winning cheeses and icecream, visit Jerusalem, drink endless cups of tea with Whanganui River Road locals, shovel coal aboard an old paddle steamer, and watch the sunset over Mt Taranaki.

WELLINGTON TO NEW PLYMOUTH

DAY ONE
Wellington to Wanganui

After two days discovering the capital city of Wellington, Bob and I are eager to get "on the road again" and Bob throatily sings this well known tune as we leave town, and travel north to Paraparaumu.

"Para para para – what?" he suddenly exclaims as he sees a sign. A quick language lesson follows – Maori vowels for dummies – before we come to a halt outside Lindale Animal Barn. Here we watch a shearing and milking demonstration but the highlight comes when Bob tries to master hand-milking a cow.

"It's not as easy as it looks," he later moans, "I only got one squirt!"

Before leaving we visit the Kapiti Cheese Shop and Factory where we sample some of their cheeses and purchase blocks of gold medal winning Aorangi and Kikorangi cheese to lunch upon later.

In the meantime a creamy Kapiti icecream keeps the hunger pangs at bay. I try the ginger-nut – it's scrumptious; Bob can't decide between the fig and honey, lemongrass and ginger, or port and prune. So – in true Bob-fashion – he takes a scoop of each.

At Waikanae we debate whether to visit the bird sanctuary on Kapiti Island, then settle upon a visit to the Nga Manu Wildlife Sanctuary. Here we walk through huge aviaries and discover NZ's unique flora and fauna in a variety of recreated habitats. Bob spots two North Island brown kiwi in the kiwi house as well as three prehistoric-looking tuatara basking in the sun.

We enjoy our picnic on an island surrounded by eels. "Here's the great-grandmother," says Bob, feeding a cracker to an enormous eel who looks like he's enjoyed a lifetime of overindulgence.

Replete we drive north on SH1 through numerous small towns: Otaki, Levin, Foxton and Bulls, where we take SH3 to Wanganui, a town nestled on the banks of the Whanganui River. Now somewhat out of the way, Wanganui was once a major tourist attraction forming part of a thriving route between Auckland and Wellington. Steamers plied the river transporting visitors from the central plateau town of Taumaranui to Wanganui; a stationary houseboat and hotel in Pipiriki accommodated guests en route. Plummeting tourist numbers in the depression years brought an end to the riverboat era, but memories of its heyday survive in the town's many original homes and historic buildings

Visitors can also recreate the experience aboard NZ's only coal-fired paddle steamer, the *PS Waimarie*. We arrive in time for the 2 pm departure and with a cheerful toot we're off. Captain Barry Thorner is at the wheel and we join engineer, Kevin Holly, and stoker, Murray Greathead below in the engine room. Bob lends a hand to shovel coal but it's excruciatingly

hot, so I retreat to the comfort of the saloon leaving Bob to discuss the *Waimarie's* original, fully restored engines.

Later we drive down Wanganui's main street and admire its many beautiful buildings including the Opera House, built in 1899, and the Sarjeant Gallery, which features many notable artworks from the 19th and 20th centuries, before checking into a B&B nestled beside the river.

We finish the day watching the sunset over distant Mt Taranaki from the top of a 33.5 metre Memorial Tower constructed at the end of WWI. The 176-step staircase helps build an appetite and we dine at Vega on Taupo Quay upon salmon and ostrich steaks before returning to our accommodation, where I (at least) enjoy a sound sleep.

DAY TWO
Wanganui to Hawera with a side trip up the Whanganui River Road

"Donna wake up," Bob whispers urgently at some ridiculous hour of the morning. He awoke at 4 am and, not wishing to disturb me (until now) read a book about the River Road. But it seems he can wait no longer, we must go to Jerusalem – without delay! And so it is that we follow the emerald Whanganui River up a route that is more like a driveway, so friendly are its inhabitants. Near Koriniti we stop and chat to a group of pig hunters who heave a glossy black boar up the riverbank. "It's a big'n," says Tex, who invites us to share in the pig which will be cooked on a spit, in true Whanganui River style.

Sadly we decline and leave tooting the horn. Bob comments on how welcoming everyone is. As we continue our drive Bob entertains me with an account of his early morning read including the Maori legend of the forming of the Whanganui River. Mt Taranaki lost a fierce battle with Mt Tongariro over the fair maiden Pihanga (a smaller mountain in the central plateau) and fled to Taranaki, carving the Whanganui River and filling it with his tears. Later, when Europeans set up farms, transport was required to get their produce into town so in 1891 the paddle steamer *Wairere* began a regular service.

When we arrive in Jerusalem, St Joseph's Church casts a mirrored image of its steeple upon the river. A Roman Catholic Mission was established here in 1854 and the late James K Baxter, an influential NZ poet, formed a community here in the 1960s and wrote the Jerusalem Sonnets. His grave is at St Joseph's where Sisters Sue, Laboure and Anna Maria, the guardians of this church and its grounds warmly welcome us. Sister Sue makes us tea and then leads us to Baxter's grave.

On our return to Wanganui we stop again on the riverbank in Koriniti to watch canoes float past. Here we meet Ann Handley, who with all the usual friendliness of Whanganui River folk, invites us in for a hot cuppa with ninety-eight-year-old Granny who has lived on the river all her life. Her earlier days were spent at a huge farm station across the river from Jerusalem and once a year she would make the long journey by paddle steamer into town. Back then it took one day to get there, one day to shop and another day to return. "They were the best days of my life," Granny tells us.

After several cups of tea and slices of fruit loaf served with lashings of Ann's homegrown

Wellington to New Plymouth: Attractions and Activities

Lindale Animal Barn: www.kapiti.org.nz
Nga Manu Wildlife Sanctuary: ngamanu.co.nz
Paddle Steamer Waimarie: www.waimarie.co.nz
St Joseph's Church: Jerusalem
The Elvis Museum: www.digitalus.co.nz/elvis/gallery.html
Hawera Water Tower: Hawera
Tawhiti Museum: www.tawhitimuseum.co.nz
The Soap Factory: Opunake, SH45
Maui Production Station: Oaonui, SH45
Tandem Surfing: Oakura, SH45

Wellington to New Plymouth: Cafés and Eateries

Vega: Cnr Taupo Quay & Victoria Ave, Wanganui
Yarrows Bakery: Main St, Manaia
Sugar Juice Café: Tasman St, Opunake
Coastal Café: 70 Tasman St, Opunake
The Fuse Factory: 47 High St, Hawera
Green Ginger Café: SH45, Oakura
Café Wunderbar: SH45, Oakura

Surfing at Oakura - Donna Blaber
below: Elvis Presley Museum - Donna Blaber

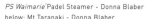

PS Waimarie Padel Steamer - Donna Blaber
below: Mt Taranaki - Donna Blaber

> And so it is that we follow the emerald Whanganui River up a route that is more like a driveway, so friendly are its inhabitants

manuka honey, mid afternoon comes all too soon. We depart for Wanganui and rejoining SH3, drive through the townships of Waverley and Patea to Hawera where we check into a motel and order a takeout meal. Although tired from his early start, Bob's jubilant. "I've never drunk that much tea or met such friendly people," he says. "Is it all a dream?"

DAY THREE
Wellington to Wanganui

In the morning Mt Taranaki is parading his magnificent Fuji-like torso in the sun as we begin our day at Kevin Wasley's Elvis Presley Museum. Kevin or 'KD' as he's known in these parts, greets us at the curb and vigorously shakes Bob's hand when he discovers that he's a fellow enthusiast.

But perhaps not as passionate – when we step inside his garage it's like a shrine, with the floors, ceiling and walls plastered in Elvis pictures, posters and newspaper cuttings. KD began his collection

in 1959 when he was 14 years old and amongst the numerous exhibits are old LP covers, signed records and albums from around the world, photos, posters, number plates, cuff links, a jumble of replica clothes and endless other memorabilia. "It's my tribute to the man," he tells us before we depart to climb up the Hawera Water Tower. From the top we have excellent views of the vibrant, green Taranaki countryside, before we drive to Tawhiti Museum, hailed as one of the best private museums in NZ.

The brainchild of ex-art teacher, Nigel Ogle, its galleries recreate many aspects of early life in South Taranaki, from the Maori-European land wars to the struggles of the dairy industry.

"It's so lifelike," says Bob as we admire Nigel's painstakingly crafted models in realistic historical settings.

We leave town on SH45, the legendary Surf Highway, which horseshoes around the coastline beneath Mt Taranaki, past several popular surfing haunts en route to New Plymouth.

In Manaia, a town centred upon an octagon-shaped roundabout and dubbed the 'bread capital' of NZ, we stop at Yarrows, a family-owned bakery which has been in operation since 1923. Their buttery hand-rolled croissants and Danish pastries are renowned and after a Danish each, we continue onto Opunake, where we meet Dave, the town's barber, after Bob (spotting the stripy barber's pole) peers through the window and announces that he's due for a cut.

While Bob attends to his grooming, I visit the eye-catching Everybody's Theatre next door where Marilyn Monroe and Charlie Chaplin grace its billboards. Movies play every Friday and Sunday night and its interior is charming, with old-style movie chairs and posters.

Then I pop along to visit Heather Baldwin at the Soap Factory, where she makes everything from scratch and gathers seaweed for her wares from the beach. Prices start at $1.25, so there's something here for everyone, even for kids looking for a nice gift for Mum.

When I return Bob's hair is under control and he's chatting to Dave about a message he discovered in a bottle. "I found it up the road," Dave tells us, "it was sent by a guy in the South African Navy." Quite a talking piece, the bottle is on display in his shop. "Lots of people

come to see it," he says.

For lunch we have delicious chicken cranberry pizzas followed by huge slabs of homemade chocolate cake at the Sugar Juice Café, then admire the town's many murals, and hunt for treasures at the Old Curiosity Shop before we leave.

In Oaonui we catch a glimmer of Taranaki's $2 billion energy industry at the Maui Production Station visitor centre before we arrive in Pungarehu. We drive through an unusual landscape of bobbly hills and cabbage trees to the Cape Egmont lighthouse where Bob takes a stunning photo of the tall beacon with Mt Taranaki in the background.

In Oakura, a famous surf beach just south of New Plymouth, Bob hires a surfboard and gear from Vertigo, while I don a wetsuit and go for a tandem surf ride with Greg Page on a custom-made four-metre surfboard. It's totally exhilarating and later as we stand on the beach drinking mugs of hot tea Greg tells us that he first learnt to surf with his father, balancing on the front of his board.

It turns out that Greg's no stranger to carrying extra bodies on his

board – he's even surfed on a 28-foot board with 13 others for the Guinness Book of Records. We check out the photographs and newspaper clippings at Vertigo before we depart for Puke Ariki in New Plymouth, a unique combination of library, museum and information centre located behind the waving Len Lye wind-wand sculpture on the waterfront.

Here we learn the stories of the region, including a rendition of Mt Taranaki's sad tale, before taking a pre-dinner stroll along the waterfront.

All of a sudden Bob stops and stares profoundly at the pounding sea. "They say Mt Taranaki's lonesome here all by himself but you know what, I think he's loving every minute of it - look at him now," he drawls.

I turn to look at Mt Taranaki's icy crown which basks in the last rays of the setting sun. He has a rosy glow and actually looks extremely content – if you believe that a mountain can find happiness.

"You know Bob," I say eventually, "I'd really have to agree." ■

Molesworth Station - Deerace Publishing

TAKE THE SCENIC ROUTE WITH APEX

100% NEW ZEALAND CAR HIRE

WWW.APEXRENTALS.COM

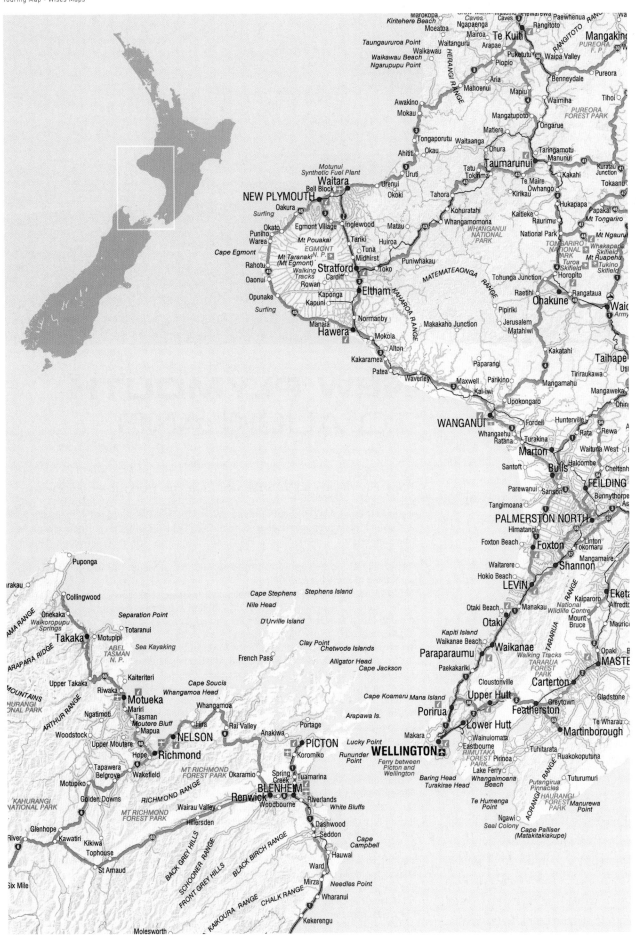

The Forgotten Highway threads its way from Taranaki through forests of beech and small villages (including the unique 'republic' of Whangamomona) to Taumarunui, located in the foothills of the Tongariro National Park. Further north, the world-famous Waitomo Glow-worm Caves were formed 30 million years ago and discovered in 1887 by Tane Tinorau and Fred Mace. South of Auckland, on the western coastline, the harbour townships of Kawhia and Raglan were once important ports prior to the advent of road and rail. Today traditional kiwi baches form the majority of dwellings but larger, architecturally designed houses verify that the west coast has become a popular lifestyle choice for many.

On our final scenic North Island drive we travel from New Plymouth to Auckland via Taumarunui, Waitomo, Kawhia and Raglan. We visit the gravesite of Billy Gumboot the goat (ex-president of Whangamomona!), float on a raft beneath galaxies of glow-worms, enjoy a cultural tour of Kawhia by boat, take a hot sandy bath at Te Puia Springs and arrive in Auckland relaxed and ready to see the scenic South Island.

NEW PLYMOUTH
TO AUCKLAND

DAY ONE
New Plymouth to Taumarunui via the Forgotten Highway

It's hard to leave New Plymouth with so much left to do. We've walked in Pukekura Park and visited the impressive rhododendron dells of Pukeiti, but the Sugar Loaf Islands Marine Park and the Taranaki Mineral Pools - where you can soak in 27,000-year-old thermal waters - remain outstanding.

"Never mind," say Bob as we exit town on SH3 to Inglewood. "It's always good to leave something to come back to."

At Lake Mangamahoe we stop for a photo of Mt Taranaki's reflection on the water's tranquil surface before continuing to the outskirts of Inglewood, where we drive up the mountain through forest bearded densely with lichen and mosses to the Dept. of Conservation information centre. Its displays prove excellent – as do the views – and after soaking up the scenery we drive on to Stratford's Clock Tower in time for the 10 am glockenspiel, where the tragedy of Shakespeare's Romeo and Juliet unfolds to the peal of bells.

After enjoying a latté in the sun we leave town on SH43, or the Forgotten Highway as it's more commonly known. Flanked by the railroad it's a heritage trail that runs from Stratford to Taumarunui and has several attractions en route including a brick kiln and boarding house, a disused coalmine, coal seams on the roadside, old bridges and tunnels, riverboat landings and several Maori heritage sites.

We pass the rustic brick kiln and at Strathmore Saddle we stop to stretch our legs and admire the views of Mt Taranaki to the west, and Mt Tongariro, Mt Ruapehu and Mt Ngauruhoe to the east.

In Whangamomona there's a pub, a café and a garage – and not a heck of a lot more at first glance. A guy in the garage gives us a friendly wave as we pass by.

"Let's stop for lunch here," says Bob pointing to M&M's Café, housed in what was once the old Australasia bank. Inside we meet Marg – one of the M's – her husband Mert, at the garage, is the other.

Within a short time we discover that this very small town has a very big heart. It's also possibly the smallest fun 'republic' on earth. Marg fills us in: "Bureaucratic bungling in '89 saw Whangamomona realigned with Wanganui instead of Taranaki and locals got a bit upset," she says, " A meeting in the pub resulted in them declaring it a republic."

Nowadays they celebrate their independence day in January in style with presidential elections. Past presidents have included Billy Gumboot the goat, who ate the oppositions votes in the '99 election but died in active service (his gravesite is now a tourist attraction overlooking the main street) and Tai, a poodle, who was top dog until an assassination attempt

left him in no mental state to rule!

In January 2005 Marg's Mert became president and a crowd of over 4000 poured into town to take part in the celebrations.

"It was all on," says Marg. "We had a sheep race down the main street, Clydesdale rides, shearing and chainsaw sculpting, wood chopping, and even an eel bath."

"An eel bath?" enquiries Bob looking startled.

"Oh yes," laughs Marg. "Some people squirmed but others seemed quite relaxed!"

Bob looks at me and shakes his head, and before we leave town we stick our heads into the pub and visit Billy Gumboot's grave.

At the Damper Falls we hike to the 85 metre waterfalls which are said to be the highest in the North Island. They spill over a horseshoe-shaped bluff into a bush-fringed pool. "Spectacular," is Bob's only comment.

We drive through the Tangarakau Gorge's magnificent podocarp forests to the Aukopae River Boat Landing, where riverboats landed cargoes of settlers, livestock and provisions before arriving in Taumarunui.

"Well," says Bob, after we've checked into our motel and sat down to a meal at a local restaurant, "It may be called the Forgotten Highway but I'm always going to remember that town!"

DAY TWO
Taumarunui to Waitomo

The morning brings showers as we head north and rejoin SH3 at Eight Mile Junction, pass through Te Kuiti, the Shearing Capital of the World, and turn off to Waitomo Caves.

En route we debate whether to: a) take a black water rafting trip (float on an inner-tube through dark caves with Waitomo Adventures), or b) take a walking tour. Bob's keen to walk while I'd rather float with Waitomo Adventures as they have an excellent reputation, but in the end, as we only have two more days in the North Island, we compromise and opt for a wetsuit-free cave adventure with Spellbound.

We join a small group at the information centre where we depart with our guide, Katy. A rocky downhill stroll leads to the Mangawhitikau Cave where we don safety helmets and enter its inky blackness. A stream runs through and there are several good examples of stalagmites and stalactites.

We board a raft and Katy instructs us to switch off the miner-lamps on our helmets. Then, as we gently float through the darkness, glow-worms begin to emit bright beams of light tinged with green. Before long countless galaxies are swirling by with such dizzying regularity that Bob comments that he feels like we're on the set of Star Trek.

And wait, there is a sound....and it's not the theme music, it's a.... waterfall?!

"Oh no," yelps Bob, "you promised we wouldn't get wet!" The roaring gets louder and louder and just as I wonder if I have actually let Bob down, Katy flicks on her safety helmet light and we disembark.

What sounded like a 12 metre waterfall is in fact only a foot high, thanks to the cave's awesome acoustics. Bob looks rather sheepish when he sees it but Katy reassures him that he's not the first to be fooled.

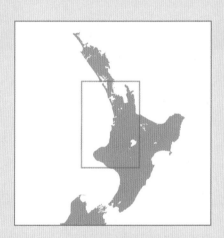

New Plymouth to Auckland:
Attractions and Activities

Pukeiti: www.pukeiti.org.nz

Stratford Clock Tower: Stratford

Blackwater Rafting:www.blackwaterrafting.co.nz

Spellbound:www.waitomospellbound.co.nz

Museum of Caves: www.waitomo-museum.co.nz

Waitomo Adventures: www.waitomo.co.nz

Waitomo Glowworm Caves: www.waitomocaves.co.nz

Lady Kawhia Tours: www.kingcountry.co.nz

Te Puia Springs: Kawhia

Bridal Veil Falls: Off Te Mata Rd, Raglan

New Plymouth to Auckland:
Cafés and Eateries

Urban Attitude Café: Broadway, Stratford

M&M's Café: SH43, Whangamomona

Waitomo Caves Hotel: Waitomo Caves Rd, Waitomo

Kawhia Seafoods: Waterfront, Kawhia

Annie's Café: Jervois St, Kawhia

Tongue & Groove: 19 Bow St, Raglan

Vinnies: 7 Wainui Rd, Raglan

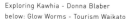

> **As we gently float through the darkness, glow-worms begin to emit bright beams of light tinged with green**

Back in Waitomo, we call into the Information Centre. It's a great place to discover the region as the adjoining Museum of Caves has an excellent display on Waitomo's 'karst' landscapes. There's also a multimedia show, Arachnocampa Luminosa, which tells the story of the NZ glow-worm.

I squeeze through the cave crawl, a simulated caving experience, and Bob gives it a go too but winds up stuck like Pooh Bear in Rabbit's hole. Fortunately for Bob – unlike the unfortunate Pooh – we manage to get him out without resorting to drastic measures.

A tad embarrassed, Bob buries himself in the history of cave exploration, while I chat to the friendly information staff about afternoon activities. The choices are endless from abseiling into the spectacular Lost World with Waitomo Adventures (it looks absolutely amazing!) to horse trekking, quad biking, hiking and an early pioneer heritage show at Woodlyn Park.

In the end Bob and I decide to check in to the grand-looking Waitomo Hotel overlooking the village and work out later what we're going to do next. A narrow staircase leads to our rooms in the original Victorian-style octagonal turret and after settling in we relax outside on lawn chairs that provide vast views over the Waitomo Valley.

Later, feeling more energetic and having enjoyed our small taste of caving in Mangawhitikau Cave, we decide to tour the Waitomo Caves which put this town on the map when they were discovered in 1887.

We join a small group and enter the cave with Richmond, a local Maori guide with an extensive knowledge of the region's geology. He tells us that Waitomo's limestone landscape was formed about 30 million years ago from the bones and shells of billions of sea creatures.

We tour the upper levels of the caves, then take the stairs down into the 46-foot-high 'cathedral', with its impressive stalactites and stalagmites. The highlight for Bob and I comes at the end with another awe-inspiring boat ride through caverns lit by millions of glow-worms.

We head back to the hotel for dinner in an atmospheric dining room complete with chandeliers. Afterwards we relax beside the log fire where we meet an elderly couple from New Plymouth who reminisce about the hotel's heydays. "It was pure luxury in the '30s," they say. "These days we keep coming back because it's just as we remember, even the wallpaper's the same!"

DAY THREE
Waitomo to Auckland

Our final day in the North Island dawns bright and clear. "Let's take the back roads through Kawhia and Raglan," says Bob, who has obviously done his research.

"What a shame," I say, "we'll miss Otorohanga's wonderful kiwi house." Bob looks suitably remorseful but clearly he's keen to make the most of our last scenic drive in the North Island.

And so we leave Waitomo driving through a dramatic karst landscape – all rolling hills and rocky outcrops – to Haggas Lookout, where we have a clear view of Mt Tongariro, Ruapehu and Ngau-

ruhoe. At Mangapohue Natural Bridge we get out and hike for ten minutes to an impressive rock archway, and do the same again at the Marokopa Falls, which plunge some 30 metres down a cliff face to the valley below.

In Te Anga we head north to Kawhia, skimming the harbour before arriving in the township itself, a thriving port in the 1850s. The sleepy village offers a couple of cafés, a general store, a takeaway, museum and it has a large wharf.

Kawhia has a rich Maori history and we spend an informative hour soaking this up aboard Lady Kawhia, with skipper Bevan Taylor. We're his only passengers today, so we ride up front and he tells us that his whanau (family) has lived in Kawhia since the Tainui waka (canoe) arrived.

We cruise past the ancient pohutukawa tree, Tangi te Korowhiti, where Hoturoa, captain of the Tainui waka, moored upon his arrival in NZ during the 14th century, and Ahurei, a small hill south of Maketu Marae, where the same vessel was later buried. Beside the carved meeting house at Maketu, we see the Kawhia home of the Maori Queen, and the site where Hoturoa established a school for 12- to 17-year-olds to teach them how to use traditional weapons.

Bevan also tells us that the first European settlers arrived here in the mid-1820s setting up flour and flax mills until the land wars in 1863, which heralded an exodus of settlers from the King Country till 1881. The harbour was also once a busy port, but today it's a

peaceful backwater popular with fishermen, and wind and kite-surfers, who we see gliding across the harbour.

Back on terrafirma we eat fresh gurnard and chips from Kawhia Seafoods, then drive out to the wild ocean beach and Te Puia Springs, where Bevan suggested we dig a hole in the sand and take a hot soak.

"I can't believe it," says Bob as we relax in our freshly dug pool, "there's no-one else here!"

Sandy but rejuvenated we continue on to Raglan. We make a brief stop at Bridal Veil Falls and hike for ten minutes to see its cascading waters, then arrive in town with salty hair and sunburned faces, blending in well with local surfers who hang out on tables outside bustling cafes. We do likewise over lattés at Tongue and Groove before summoning up the energy to peruse Raglan's wealth of studios and arty design stores including Jet, Kanuka, the Bow Street Gallery and Scintilla, and fine old buildings such as the Harbour View Hotel.

SH22 leads us north on back roads to Tuakau and we cut across to the Bombay Hills, where from the top we watch the sunset over Auckland. The golden glow of the incoming tide sweeps its way up the harbour and as day fades into night, millions of tiny lights turn on, one after the other, illuminating the shape of isthmus below.

"Gee," says Bob, "It's beautiful. How can the South Island get any better than this?" ■

Manukau Harbour - Deerace Publishing

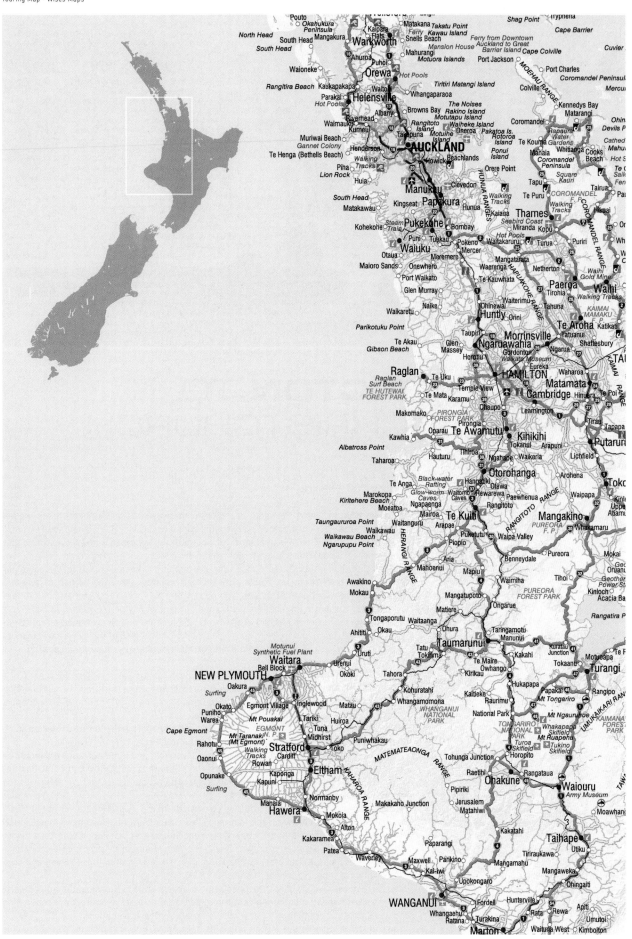

From the moment you disembark from the inter-island ferry in Picton after cruising through breathtaking Queen Charlotte Sound, there's no doubt in any visitor's mind that the South Island is very special. SH1 takes us south to Blenheim, NZ's premier wine growing region, then follows a rocky, kelp-strewn shoreline to Kaikoura, where snowy mountains plunge dramatically into the sea. Amid this stunning coastal alpine scenery, a wealth of eco-tourism oriented activities are on offer, from whale watching to seal snorkelling and much more! We take three days to travel from Picton to Christchurch. We sample the award-winning wines of the region, dine with our jolly kiwi-Italian hosts, join an awe-inspiring whale watch tour, relish the flavour of succulent Kaikoura crayfish, visit a lavender distillery and swim with dolphins that are so playful and friendly, Bob can't believe that they're wild!

PICTON TO CHRISTCHURCH

DAY ONE
Picton to Blenheim

The drive from the Ferry Terminal in Picton to the vineyards of Blenheim takes around twenty minutes – especially when a keen wine connoisseur, like Bob, is behind the wheel. "Stay on the LEFT!" I warn (as I always do) whenever we approach a new town. But to give credit where it's due, Bob's taken to right-hand drive like a duck to water!

In Blenheim we find there's more than vineyard-hopping to keep us amused. We begin our exploration at the Millennium Public Art Gallery, then walk through The Forum, where a lively market atmosphere permeates, and relax in the sun over a reviving latté before taking a stroll through the immaculately groomed gardens of Seymour Square.

A short drive leads to the Marlborough Provincial Museum and Beavertown, a replica village of old Blenheim, and here we soak up local history. It's part of the Brayshaw Museum Park complex, which is also home to a vintage farm machinery museum displaying rows of faithfully restored tractors.

En route to Montana, we visit Prenzel Distillery and Tasting Room where we meet Chris Steadman, who presses a taster of butterscotch schnapps with a 'lair' of butterscotch cream into our eager hands. It's delicious and there's also a variety of brandies, schnapps, infused olive oils and chocolate liqueurs on offer.

Bob picks up a bottle of butterscotch schnapps while I depart with a bottle of Marlborough Sauvignon Blanc Vinegar, wood-aged in oak in the traditional Orleans method.

"Perfect with blue cod," I say to Bob as we drive through the striking entrance of Montana's Brancott Winery. Many of Montana's leading labels are produced at Brancott Estate including Deutz Marlborough Cuvee, the winery's specialty, produced in partnership with the French House of Deutz.

Seated at Brancott's café-restaurant we peruse the menu. It provides a variety of fresh, Marlborough-inspired dishes, each teamed with a matching wine. Bob enjoys a deliciously fresh salad while I (motivated by my earlier vinegar purchase) feast upon blue cod fillets.

After lunch we take a guided tour, which departs from Montana's visitor centre every hour from 10 am to 3 pm. It's an ideal introduction to NZ's premier viticultural region and concludes with a tasting in a private room.

Later, armed with a copy of the free local wine map, we drive to Renwick, the hub of Marlborough's wine growing country where the region's high sunshine hours, long cool nights and low summer rainfall provide near-perfect grape-growing conditions.

"It would take a week to see all the vineyards here," says Bob, deciding in the end that we should visit Cloudy Bay, home of the legendary Cloudy Bay Sauvignon Blanc, and Grove Mill

where, as well as wine tastings, there's a 'vine library' and an art gallery.

Our last port of call is the magnificent, Tuscan-inspired Highfield Estate on Brookby Road. Situated on a crest overlooking the vineyards of the Omaka and Wairau Valleys, the views from its tower are stunning and this, combined with its small but select range of fine wines, makes it one of Marlborough's most popular wineries. In February wine-lovers gather near here for the annual BMW Wine Marlborough Festival which celebrates local wine.

All graped out – not for the first time on our circumnavigation of NZ – we retreat to the mud-brick cottage at Uno Piu and after a refreshing swim in the pool join Gino Rocco, our kiwi-Italian ex-chef host, at his dinner table.

Our meal begins with tasty blue-cheese fettuccine – made with Gino's own homemade pasta – followed by lamb with more than a hint of mint and garlic, and fresh garden vegies. Local wine is matched to each course, and dessert, a rich amaretto-infused tiramisu, is followed by Gino's favourite tipple, Italian limoncino.

After a few rounds of the latter Gino cheerfully tells Bob that he met his wife Heather on her big OE. "I was her walking, talking souvenir," laughs Gino. "We met in a kitchen and luckily I like it because I've been there ever since."

"He's a man after my own heart," says Bob before we retire, "but he uses a lot more garlic!"

DAY TWO
Blenheim to Kaikoura

After a hearty breakfast of deliciously light crepes served with blueberries, cream and maple syrup, we somewhat sadly bid Gino farewell and drive south on SH1 through a thirsty landscape to Seddon, where lush, regimented rows of vines cover its slopes.

We've had our fill of wine – and the boot is crammed with bottles – so we continue on past the salt works at Lake Grassmere to Wharanui, where the road meets the Pacific Ocean and follows the railway line south to The Store at Kekerengu. It's midway between Kaikoura and Blenheim and here we pause for refreshment, sipping flat whites on the terrace just metres from the shore.

Revived, we continue on the road that hugs the rocky, kelp-lined coastline to the tiny township of Rakautara, where Nin's Bin, a caravan embedded in the rocks by the sea, sells freshly harvested and cooked crayfish to passersby.

Further on at Ohau Point NZ fur seals bask on the rocks. "Look," says Bob, pointing to a seal flapping its flipper at a fly, "he's waving to me!"

"Pace yourself," I say, as he snaps merrily away, "there's loads more to see yet...sperm whales, Dusky dolphins, Royal albatross and even the endangered Hector's dolphin if we're lucky."

"Why do they congregate here?," asks Bob as we return to the car, and I explain about the Hikurangi Trough, a huge, submarine chasm complete with plains, ancient volcanoes and gorges just off the coast near Kaikoura. Here warm northern waters mix with a nutrient-rich Antarctic flow and its upwellings provide a rich source of food, attracting a wealth of marine life.

Arriving in Kaikoura we fortify ourselves with wholesome seafood chowder served with home-baked bread at Hislops, a popular organic café on SH1, then after confirming our whale watching cruise with Whale Watch Kaikoura we drive through town to the information centre.

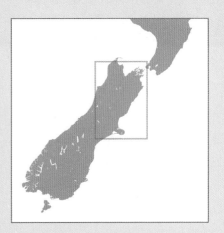

Picton to Christchurch:
Attractions and Activities

Millenium Public Art Gallery: Blenheim
Marlborough Museum: www.marlboroughmuseum.org.nz
Prenzel Distillery: www.prenzel.com
Cloudy Bay Winery: www.cloudybay.co.nz
Grove Mill Winery: www.grovemill.co.nz
Whale Watch Kaikoura: www.whalewatch.co.nz
Kaikoura Wine Company: www.kaikourawines.co.nz
Maori Leap Caves: Kaikoura
Dolphin Encounter: www.dolphin.co.nz
Lavendyl Lavender Farm: www.lavenderfarm.co.nz

Picton to Christchurch:
Cafés and Eateries

Montana Brancott Winery: Riverlands, SH1, Blenheim
Highfield Estate Winery: Brookby Rd, RD2, Renwick
The Store: SH1, Kekerengu
Nins Bin: SH1, Rakautara
Hislops: SH1, Kaikoura
Mussel Boys: SH1, Kaikoura
The Craypot: 70 Westend, Kaikoura

> " Silently we watch this great
> mammal re-oxygenate against
> a dramatic mountain backdrop
> as the sun begins to set "

From the acclaimed whale watching tours, to swimming with Dusky dolphins, albatross watching, snorkelling, diving, sea kayaking, and rides in glass-bottomed boats, the town offers a marine-based activity for everyone.

For landlubbers there's the local arts and crafts trail; the Maori Leap Caves; wine tasting on the decks of the Kaikoura Wine Company overlooking the ocean; the District Museum; and horse trekking or golf – just to name a few options!

We sit on Kaikoura's shingle beach admiring the view of the jagged ranges which plummet to the sea and watching local fishermen camped on deck chairs pull in sizeable snapper. Bob walks over for a look-see and then we drive up the rocky Kaikoura peninsula past historic Fyffe House to the Kaikoura Wildlife Refuge.

It's a popular place to view seals – and to swim with them, as we discover after scrambling over twisted limestone rocks to watch a group of snorkellers. "They're really playful," an American backpacker tells Bob as she emerges from the water, "curious and friendly."

It's late afternoon when we check into a B&B on the outskirts of town, before joining our whale watch tour and travelling out to sea aboard Aoraki, an 18-metre catamaran. A large screen shows our depth and we watch in awe as we pass over the continental shelf and the depth changes from 60 metres to a radical 1236!

Captain Hama locates a whale's position on the GPS, then turns off the engines and listens on the hydrophone for its rhythmic, clicking sonar. We stand on the viewing decks scouring the water.

"Thaaarrrr she blows," cries Bob suddenly, pointing to a whale that surfaces with a spurt of misty vapour.

Silently we watch this great mammal re-oxygenate against a dramatic mountain backdrop as the sun begins to set. Our guide, Gemma, tells us he's a young sperm whale. They often frequent this coast and feast upon its abundant food supply.

Suddenly to our right another huge column of spray is blown sky-high as a second whale empties its lungs. Captain Hama monitors its breathing to make sure he's relaxed and happy with our presence. "It's Te Ake," says Gemma, recognising his prominent dorsal fin, "he likes the boats."

Our first whale slowly lowers its blowhole into the water, flicks its graceful tail, and departs. We watch Te Ake until he finally does the same, flicking his tail with a flourish as if to bid us farewell before disappearing with the sun. Our boat returns to base and after a delicious meal of succulent Kaikoura crayfish at The Craypot, we return to our B&B and with Te Ake's plume-blowing firmly etched in our memories fall into a peaceful slumber.

DAY THREE
Kaikoura to Christchurch

At breakfast Bob asks if I fancy a swim with the Dusky dolphins. "You never know, we might see another whale too," he says enthusiastically.

At Dolphin Encounter's base we don wetsuits and, after a bus ride to South Bay, board a boat and travel along the shore. Before long we see our first pod of Dusky dolphins, but since they are resting

near the shore, we continue to deeper waters where another group dances upon the ocean.

"Play with them," instructs our guide, Mark, as we dive off the stern one-by-one. "They'll go away if they get bored so I want to see lots of ducking and diving," he says.

As Bob and I swim away from the boat I'm thankful for my wetsuit. Suddenly, from somewhere in the green murky depths comes a call. "Eeeeeeeeeeee." It sends waves of shivers up my spine and Bob gives me a startled look as seawater fills my snorkel and I blow it out like a submerging orca.

In no time at all there's company - a fast moving shape slides beneath. Panic is rapidly replaced with excitement as two Dusky dolphins come into view. They swim in unison and scrutinise Bob and I in our strange rubbery suits.

One dolphin leaves, obviously concluding that we're no fun, but the other stays, peering at us playfully. We both roll and he immediately copies, and so we do it again. For a few minutes we twist around and around in the water until it's hard to say who's copying whom! In a final farewell he leaps up out of the water into a perfect arc and back down with a sleek splash. Bob gives it a go but fails dismally; the result is a resounding belly flop and laughter from the boat.

It's super-exciting but we sit out the next round and instead watch these acrobatic dolphins from the boat. Bob's got his camera ready

and within moments they're leaping out of the water and showing off their beautiful luminous white bellies. As they become more excited their tricks increase; before long they're spinning, side-slapping and somersaulting both forwards and back.

It's hard to leave, but a hot shower at the base is in order, as is a late lunch. We eat chilli mussels at Mussel Boys, then follow this up with a little retail therapy at Lavendyl Lavender Farm before leaving town.

There are five and a half acres of lavender and after we've explored the gardens Gary Morris kindly demonstrates how the oil is extracted using steam. Their small store provides a variety of handcrafted lavender products for sale, from lavender-infused olive oil, to soaps, and lavender and rosemary massage cream. I buy a couple of treats and we head south towards the garden city of Christchurch, following the coast then travelling inland to Cheviot and on through the wine-growing region of Waipara to Amberley.

Bob's editing his photos (apparently the waving seal turned out well) and as we cross a long bridge over the braided Waimakariri River he suddenly starts waving his camera in front of my face and hopping with excitement. "Wow, this one's right out of the water!" he shouts, as I crane my neck to keep my eyes on the road.

Bob shakes his head. "Those Dusky dolphins are just amazing," he says, clicking rapidly through his photos, "I wouldn't believe they're wild if I hadn't seen it for myself!" ▪

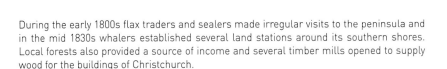

AKAROA

A scenic one and a half hour's drive from Christchurch leads to Akaroa on the Banks Peninsula, a quaint town steeped in European history with more than a touch of French charm.

Captain James Cook and the crew aboard the Endeavour were the first Europeans to sight the peninsula in February 1770. Cook, deceived by the peninsula's low-lying marshes and high headlands, mistakenly recorded it as Banks Island after his botanist Joseph Banks. It wasn't until some 40 years later, when a mariner sought a non-existent sea passage, that the mistake was discovered and charts were corrected.

In 1838 Jean Francois Langlois, the captain of a whaling ship, purchased land from local Maori and the French began a determined effort to start a colony in the Pacific. Langlois returned to France and made arrangements for French settlers to colonise the land, but while the immigrants were en route the English were already in the process of establishing sovereignty over New Zealand following the signing of the Treaty of Waitangi.

Six days before Captain Lavaud arrived in Akaroa Harbour with his cargo of 57 French and German migrants, the British flag was raised at Akaroa's Green Point. The settlers, having travelled such a long way, chose to stay regardless. They built houses and planted their gardens with fruit and nut trees, and with rose bushes that had survived the long sea journey. In 1843, after several years of debate, an agreement was finally reached which saw the French accepting British rule of law in New Zealand and relinquishing any claims to jurisdiction.

During the early 1800s flax traders and sealers made irregular visits to the peninsula and in the mid 1830s whalers established several land stations around its southern shores. Local forests also provided a source of income and several timber mills opened to supply wood for the buildings of Christchurch.

It wasn't until April 1850 however that the first British settlers arrived aboard the SS Monarch. From this point onwards the township of Akaroa was established with the French located at the north end of the beach and the British at the south end. A small bay divided the settlements.

Today evidence of the town's Gallic past remains in many of the street signs and historic buildings. Keen historians will find much of the town's varied and colourful history on display at the Akaroa Museum. There are Maori taonga (treasures), relics from its whaling past, and the museum incorporates several historical buildings including the Customs House at Daly's Wharf, the old courthouse, and the Langlois-Eteveneaux House, built in the early 1840s and one of the oldest houses in the South Island. A 20-minute audio-visual relates the complete history of the town.

The Akaroa Historic Area Walk also provides an insight into Akaroa's history, following the town's narrow winding streets past old colonial cottages, churches and other mid-nineteenth century buildings which reflect the influence of the early French and British settlers. Guide booklets detailing the walk are available at the museum or from the Akaroa Information Centre.

Alternatively Akaroa's ambience can be soaked up while relaxing at one of its many seaside cafes overlooking the deep, still waters of the harbour. Here all sorts of fishing, pleasure and charter boats travel to and fro on the changing tide. Fresh catch of the day can be sampled at these tables by the sea as can some of the excellent local Akaroa wine.

Akaroa is well known for its artisan products and there's some great boutique stores offering local arts and crafts. You can also meet artists in their home studios and, while en route, discover local gourmet foods such as olive products at The Olive Grove and specialty cheese at nearby Barrys Bay Cheese.

Akaroa Harbour is a deep sea-filled crater, which creates a fascinating marine environment. Informative harbour cruises are offered aboard the Black Cat, taking visitors to historical sites and offering opportunities to spot fur seals, blue penguins, Hector's dolphins and several species of sea birds. The company also provides the only opportunity in New Zealand to swim with the unique Hector's (or NZ) dolphin, one of the world's smallest and rarest species with a total population of around 6-7000 individuals. Tours depart daily from the Akaroa wharf. ■

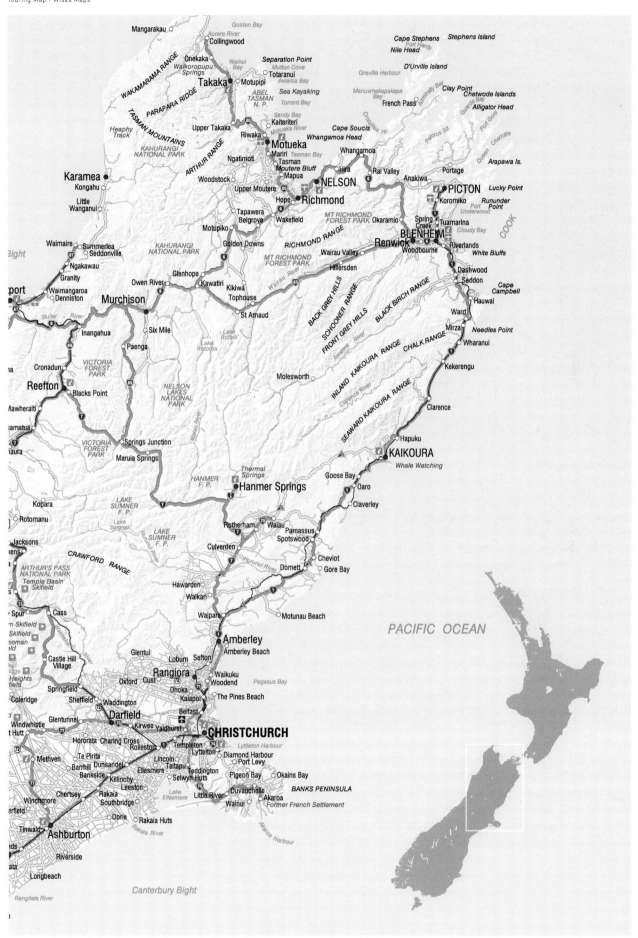

PACIFIC OCEAN

THERMAL SPRINGS & SPAS

Thermal springs and spas are found throughout New Zealand, as a result of the country's position on the Pacific Rim of Fire, a belt of seismic and volcanic activity which forms an arc around the Pacific Ocean basin. Rotorua, a hotbed of thermal activity with its boiling mud pools, spouting geysers and sulphurous rock pools, is well known for its natural spas. These include Wai Ora at Hells Gate, the Blue Baths and the Polynesian Spa on the lakefront – just to name a few. At other unique locations throughout the North Island you can dig your own spa right on the beach. Try this out at Te Puia Springs in Kawhia and at Coromandel's Hot Water Beach, or wallow in a naturally heated stream at the somewhat unfortunately named Kerosene Creek, south of Rotorua.

But the North Island doesn't have a monopoly on New Zealand's thermal spa activity. At Maruia Springs, deep in the heart of the Lewis Pass in the South Island, each pool is a perfectly formed tarn built from the smoothest of river rocks. Gold miners enjoyed these mineral-rich waters, which are thought to be particularly beneficial for detoxifying and softening the skin. No chemicals are added to change its composition, so the colour palette of the pools changes daily, ranging from crystal clear to milky, and through to almost black. For hardy

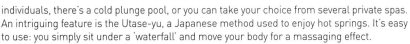

The Maori knew of Hanmer Springs and legends tell of Tamatea, whose canoe was wrecked off the Otago coast. To save his party from freezing he called upon the mountains of Tongariro and Ngauruhoe in the north for help. They sent flames down the Whanganui River and across to Nelson where they rose into the air and landed at Hanmer Springs. It wasn't until 1859 that Europeans chanced upon the springs, but Hanmer's development was hindered by its inaccessibility and the first bathing shed, made from iron, wasn't erected until 1879.

The springs, well known for their recuperative powers, have shared a close history with nearby Queen Mary Hospital. They were used to assist soldiers returning from the war and have provided relief for the arthritic and disabled.

Nowadays they are a fantastic place to spend a day with the family or relax and indulge yourself with a hot soak followed by a relaxing therapeutic massage or beauty treatment at Health, Body and Mind. Treatments include Swiss and sports massage, detoxifying body wraps and aromatic facials.

To enter the pools visitors can choose from a range of group, family and return passes, or purchase a Concession Card which allows ten adult, or 20 child admissions.

For more information please view www.hanmersprings.co.nz or from within NZ phone 0800 442 663.

individuals, there's a cold plunge pool, or you can take your choice from several private spas. An intriguing feature is the Utase-yu, a Japanese method used to enjoy hot springs. It's easy to use: you simply sit under a 'waterfall' and move your body for a massaging effect.

In the stunning alpine village of Hanmer Springs, 90 minutes' drive north of Christchurch, the award-winning Hanmer Springs Thermal Pools and Spa is spacious and well laid out. There are seven open-air thermal pools, three sulphur pools and four private pools, as well as a sauna, steam rooms, a freshwater heated pool, a family activity pool with water-slides, and a picnic area and licensed café.

The pools range in temperature from 33-42 degrees Celsius and are surrounded by a beautifully landscaped natural environment with native plantings. There are four large outdoor rock pools connected by a thermal stream. The completely natural sulphur pools contain no chlorine and leave your skin feeling soft and silky. Hanmer Springs' naturally therapeutic waters contain a wide variety of minerals including sulphur, sodium chloride, calcium, carbonates, magnesium and potassium, and are said to be particularly beneficial to those suffering from arthritis or similar ailments. ■

The Southern Alps provide a pristine playground for New Zealanders and nowhere more so than at Mt Hutt, an easy two-hour drive from Christchurch. Travelling south the road hugs the foothills to the quintessential country towns of Geraldine and Fairlie, before ascending into Mackenzie country where the turquoise-blue waters of Lake Tekapo and Lake Pukaki contrast sharply with the dry, rocky hinterland. SH80 leads to Mount Cook, NZ's highest mountain, and to the rumbling Tasman Glacier, with its lake embedded in a vast lunar-like landscape. Further south the popular lakeside resorts of Wanaka and Queenstown, both situated beside sparkling lakes in a stunning alpine setting, provide endless opportunities for adventure activities.

We take three days to explore the route from Christchurch to Queenstown and begin the journey with an unexpected snowboard lesson at Mt Hutt. We buy new jumpers in Geraldine, spend the evening with locals at a country cinema, enjoy a scenic flight over Mt Cook, taste 500-year-old ice from the Tasman Glacier, sunbathe in Wanaka, explore Arrowtown and relax on the shores of Queenstown's Lake Wakatipu wondering where we should begin!

CHRISTCHURCH
TO QUEENSTOWN

DAY ONE
Christchurch to Geraldine

It's 10 am at Mt Hutt, and Bob and I have miraculously caught the tail end of what has been a wonderfully long ski season. Two and a half hours ago we left Christchurch and now – quite unexpectedly – we're in a snowboard class on the slopes of Mt Hutt. We watch in awe as others sashay skilfully past, totally at ease with their boards.

We haven't connected with ours in quite the same manner, but fortunately there are several other beginners sharing the same dilemma. However the younger members of our group are picking it up depressingly fast. Our instructor, James Harding, is patient even though it's hard to teach old dogs new tricks. "Focus on where you're going and your board will follow," James tells Bob. It's good advice, and when the lesson ends we feel confident of the basics.

The mountain air and exercise has worked up an appetite and so we drive back across the rushing Rakaia Gorge to the Terrace Downs High Country Resort, nestled in the foothills of the Southern Alps by the Rakaia River. The championship 18-hole links style golf course sports nine lakes and 70 bunkers but we're not here for a round, rather to enjoy lunch and après-ski in the clubhouse restaurant where everyone's welcome. Our table overlooks the course and mountains and after dining on rich venison we head downstairs to the spa pools which feature massive bi-fold windows framing views of the mountains – and nine holes of golf!

Refreshed we leave and drive to Geraldine, a pretty town nestled beside the Talbot Forest on the banks of the Waihi River. Our first port of call after checking into our accommodation is at the Giant Jersey, where made to measure garments are knitted in fine Perendale, Mohair or Merino wool. After a cool morning on the slopes Bob decides he needs a new jumper.

Fortunately Michael and Gillian Linton's shop boasts around 1000 pre-made jerseys on its shelves, so there's plenty from which to choose.

"Do you think that would fit?" Bob teases Gillian pointing to a colossal jumper that is pinned to the wall. It was made in 1991, and the Lintons were later awarded a mention in the Guinness Book of Records for the largest ever.

"It's the only jersey we have that really is 'one size fits all'," laughs Gillian as we leave.

Geraldine is full of artisans. We visit the Belanger-Taylor Glass Studio, where Denise, a famous Canadian glass blower, and her husband Stephen work side by side, and then return to Chocolate Fellman's on the main street. Here qualified chocolatier, Rene Fellman,

makes the finest chocolate using specially imported gourmet couverture. Bob's eyes boggle at the array on offer which includes a Kiwi classic – chocolate fish!

Many of Geraldine's creative products come in edible form and so – munching chocolate fish – we visit Talbot Forest Cheese where cheesemaker Paul Fitzsimons crafts his tasty wares, followed by Barker Fruit Processors and the Honey Corner Shop.

In the end we taste so many samples that dinner is an inhouse snack before we depart to watch an art house comedy screened on an old Ermemanm Model II projector at Geraldine's classic country-style cinema.

It's run by Barry and Anthea McLauchlan and we're greeted on the doorstep by 'Reverend Barry' as he's known around town. He ushers us inside and offers a choice of seating: a cozy couch downstairs, or a regular seat up top. We choose a two-seater and watch as tracksuit wearing country-types fill the room, and the movie begins.

About halfway through, it suddenly flickers, then stops. Thinking the projector has broken down Bob whispers, "Let's go," just as 'Reverend' Barry booms out "INTERMISSION!" and in rolls the wine and cheese.

It's really kind of bizarre and Bob's absolutely delighted, "What a great idea," he says, "We should do this back home!"

Later on as we bid newly-met friends farewell Bob thanks Barry who's standing on the steps waving farewell. "It's the most fun I've ever had at a cinema!" he says.

"Ah good," says Barry, "country folks round here like a bit of a catch up."

DAY TWO
Geraldine to Mt Cook

After a slower start to the day we sit above Fairlie admiring the view of the Southern Alps. We stop for a latte at the town's Old Library Café, then stretch our legs around its Heritage Museum.

But Bob's keen to get into the mountains and so we depart, ascending through Burkes Pass to the vast open landscape of Mackenzie country and the Church of the Good Shepherd at Lake Tekapo, where we arrive amid a flurry of tour buses.

"Wow," says Bob, as we wait it out before we enter the church, "I'm sure glad we're travelling by car and can take our time."

The church, constructed from stones gathered locally, was built as a memorial to the pioneers of the Mackenzie Country. Nearby, the bronze statue of a sheep dog, erected in memory of all high-country mustering dogs, gazes longingly at the turquoise-blue lake. "I think he wants a swim," says Bob.

There's a long line of eateries on Tekapo's main street serving a variety of international fare, but we choose to picnic in the park beside the beautiful lake. Lunch includes fresh fruit and chutney from Barkers, and crackers and smoky manuka cheese from Talbot Forest Cheese.

Then we depart and drive the alternate scenic route to Lake Pukaki along the Tekapo Canal Road, stopping at the Mount Cook Salmon Farm en route.

Here these tasty fish are farmed in pens. We take a self-guided tour and discover that the

Christchurch to Queenstown: Attractions and Activities

Mt Hutt Ski Field: www.nzski.com
Terrace Downs: www.terracedowns.co.nz
Giant Jersey: www.giantjersey.co.nz
Geraldine Heritage Cinema: Geraldine
Mt Cook Salmon Farm: www.mtcooksalmon.com
Mt Cook Ski Planes: www.mtcookskiplanes.com
Glacier Explorers: www.glacierexplorers.co.nz
Lakes District Museum: www.museumqueenstown.com
TSS Earnslaw: www.realjourneys.co.nz
Skyline Gondola: www.skyline.co.nz

Christchurch to Queenstown: Cafés and Eateries

Riverside Café, 45c Talbot St, Geraldine
Berry Barn Bakery: 76 Talbot St, Geraldine
Old Library Café: 7 Allandale Rd, Fairlie
Glentanner Restaurant: SH80, Mt Cook
Panorama Restaurant: The Hermitage, Mt Cook
Habebes: Wakatipu Arcade, Rees St, Queenstown
Café de Paris: Earnslaw Wharf, Beach St, Queenstown

> We gain excellent views
> of the lower Tasman Glacier,
> a rock-strewn river of ice
> rumbling through a vast
> lunar-like landscape

smallest smelt are located downstream and are moved upstream as they grow, pen by pen, until they reach 'death row' at two years of age. Fresh salmon can be purchased, or you can catch your own on supplied rods. Bob's tempted but instead chats to a local on the bank who fishes for canny rainbow and brown trout dining on the salmon's leftovers. "I've caught more than one 12-pounder here," he tells Bob.

We continue to the Mt Cook Lookout where Aoraki's snowy crown rises majestically above Lake Pukaki, then drive up SH80 to the tiny alpine village of Mount Cook, through scenery so vast, it's over-whelming. "I feel dwarfed," says Bob.

At Mount Cook we check into the Hermitage, where our rooms provide amazing picture-postcard views of Mt Cook and Mt Sefton through enormous floor-to-ceiling windows. Then we head downstairs to the information desk where we discover there's a wealth of activities from scenic flights, heli-hiking, glacier exploration and rock climbing to 4wd journeys and lots of popular hikes including climbing the summit of Mt Cook (3754 metres) with experienced guides.

"I don't know about climbing Mt Cook, but a scenic flight sounds good," says Bob to the girl at the tour desk, who books us in on the next flight.

We spend some time at the Dept. of Conservation information centre learning about local flora and fauna, then check onto our Mount Cook Ski Planes flight, the only company licensed to land fixed-wing aircraft on the Tasman Glacier. After taking off from its tiny airport and circling Mt Cook, hydraulic skis provide a safe snow landing on the glacier, and we jump out to soak up the absolutely breath-taking scenery. Bob clicks away furiously and, after throwing a few snowballs around, we climb back on board for a unique ski take-off experience, then land back in the valley below.

Later, from the Hermitage's ambient and aptly named Panorama Restaurant, we watch the sun set over the mountains and dine, most fittingly, upon delectable Mt Cook Salmon.

DAY THREE
Mt Cook to Queenstown

The morning dawns damp and grey. "The mountains are gone," says Bob mournfully. Nevertheless we make our way early to the Blue Lakes and the Tasman Glacier View track, a 40-minute return walk from the carpark. At the lookout we gain excellent views of the lower Tasman Glacier, a rock-strewn river of ice rumbling through a vast lunar-like landscape.

"It looks forbidding," says Bob, as we return to join our Glacier Explorers tour of the lake. Our guide, Kylie Wakelin, settles our group aboard a Mac boat, then we motor alongside one of several floating icebergs. "It's made from pure water and snow that fell over 500 years ago," she says breaking some off so we can have a taste. Bob's neighbour, a Japanese chap, is prepared for the occasion. He whips out a hip flask of whiskey and a mug, adds ancient ice, and shares this heady brew with Bob as we continue across a silty, milky-grey surface to the glacier's impressive bluff which begrudgingly yields its melt to the glacier lake.

There's a medley of sound: the steady drip of melting ice, loud cracking, rumbles, creaks and splashes, as muddy ice slumps to the water leaving gaping wounds that emanate electrifying shades of blue.

It's 10 am before we begin our four-hour drive to Queenstown. As we rejoin Lake Pukaki the sky clears, but Mt Cook is completely shrouded by cloud. "Lucky we flew yesterday," says Bob.

On Twizel's Lake Ruataniwha we pass rowers, and shortly after Omarama we drive through the dramatic mountain landscape of the Lindis Pass. In Tarras we consider our lunch options, but decide to continue to Wanaka where we eat at the information centre's café nestled amongst poplars and deciduous trees on the lake's southern shores.

Bob collects tons of brochures on Queenstown's many attractions, then we soak up more sun at peaceful Glendhu Bay before resuming our journey. We take an alternate route to Queenstown, via the Cardrona Valley Rd where we stop to photograph the historic Cardrona Hotel. There are a number of activities to indulge in: horse riding, quad biking, and monster trucks and rally car rides, but we continue on through the dry tussock-filled landscape to a lookout point which offers excellent views of the mountains and Lake Hayes.

Descending, we turn off for Arrowtown, an old goldmining town nestled on the banks of the Arrow River. A wide leafy boulevard leads to this quaint town which we explore on foot, marvelling at its wealth of original cottages, shops, saloons and churches from the gold-mining period.

At the Lakes District Museum we see fascinating displays detailing the various gold-mining methods used in Arrow River and then we explore the Arrowtown Chinese settlement on the far side of town. Here also there's plenty to keep visitors amused, from playing a round at the Millbrook Golf Course to hiking, hot air ballooning, horse riding, hang gliding, parapenting as well as 4wd tours up the river to the ruins of Macetown, a goldmining ghost town.

But we're bound for Queenstown, and after driving over Edith Cavell Bridge – as the Shotover Jet skims the canyon walls beneath – we arrive in Queenstown where a charged atmosphere lingers in the crisp mountain air. Visitors join queues snaking from booking offices, while others relax outside busy cafés and bars and fill in time writing postcards before their next adrenaline-pumping activity.

We park down by the peaceful lake and sit on its shores admiring the view: trees reflect in the clear blue waters of Lake Wakatipu; The Remarkables and Cecil and Walter Peaks pierce a golden sky. The TSS Earnslaw - a coal-fired, twin-screw steamer - toots its departure to Walter Peak high country station and chugs across the lake, while behind us the Skyline Gondola almost ascends vertically to Bob's Peak, where a beautiful panorama awaits. The distant cry of punters on its 800-metre-long luge adds an air of excitement, and faint screams can be heard from the direction of the Ledge Bungy.

"Well," says Bob finally, after flicking several times through a thick wad of brochures, "Where do we begin?" ■

Adventure Capital of the World. A mighty title for a small town nestled on the shores of Lake Wakatipu but one that has been well earned. Upon arrival adventure seekers soon discover that whether you're into high adrenaline-pumping activities like bungy jumping, skydiving, jet boating, whitewater rafting, parapenting, and rally driving, or prefer milder forms of adventure entertainment such as luging, ballooning, four wheel driving, mountain biking or horse trekking, Queenstown offers something for everyone!

If your pulse quickens at the thought of throwing yourself off a bridge or platform high above the ground attached only by a single rubber band, then you'll be astounded by the range of bungy options that are on offer in Queenstown.

There's the 43-metre Kawerau Suspension Bridge bungy, where spectators look on from A. J. Hackett's brand-spanking new Bungy Centre which melds into the rock walls of the canyon; the 47-metre Ledge perched high on Bob's Peak, 400-metres above Queenstown and offering stunning views; the 102-metre Pipeline Bungy accessible only by a four wheel drive expedition through the scenically breathtaking Skippers Canyon; and the staggering 134-metre Nevis Highwire Bungy, the newest jump in town!

In the canyons beneath the Edith Cavell Bridge an adventure activity of a different ilk takes place on the Shotover Jet, where expert drivers put these famous 'Big Red' jet boats through their paces, twisting through narrow canyons, skimming past rocky outcrops and completing full 360-degree turns while spectators look on in wide-eyed wonder!

The rugged beauty and unspoiled grandeur of the upper reaches of the Shotover River also provide the setting for extreme whitewater rafting excitement; while the slightly tamer Kawarau River provides an exhilarating ride and a great introduction to whitewater rafting for first time rafters.

QUEENSTOWN ACTION

There are four rapids to negotiate including the final (and unforgettable) 400-metre Dog Leg rapid, and Kawerau rafters will gain an unusual perspective of bungy jumpers plummeting from the Kawerau Suspension Bridge.

Others hit the sky to 'feel the fear but do it anyway' stepping out into thin air on a tandem skydive. At 4,500 metres, travelling towards the ground at a staggering 200 kph, total sensory overload is reached and it makes little difference that you're harnessed to an experienced, qualified Jumpmaster and using state of the art safety equipment!

Ballooners, hang gliders and parapenters also fill the skies above Queenstown, and helicopters zoom back and forth transporting visitors to nearby Lord of the Rings filming locations. Others explore the historic Skippers Canyon on exciting four wheel drive tours that snake along a treacherously narrow trail with deep vertical drops to the vivid ice-blue Shotover River. There's the option then to raft the river, leap from the Pipeline bungy, or mountain-bike the 1860s pack track, once the only route into this isolated region.

Four wheel drive tours are also provided on a rugged route up the Arrow River, where several deep river crossings are negotiated en route to Macetown, a ghost town where hundreds of miners once flocked when alluvial gold was discovered in the Arrow River in 1862. Nearby at Xtreme Rally in the Cardrona Valley punters can zoom around a purpose-built track, sliding sideways through corners and reaching speeds of up to 160km/h on a range of rides, rated mild through to wild! Kids can join in the action too, racing 50cc Suzuki Quadmaster bikes around a specialised track; while stunt man Ian Soanes provides precarious rides aboard his giant Monster Trucks.

Other ways to explore the Cardrona Valley are on a quad bike tour at Criffel Peak Safaris or on horseback at Backcountry Saddle Expeditions, where treks range from two hours to a full day. Walter Peak High Country Farm on the far side of Queenstown's Lake Wakatipu also provides horse treks; to get there you must board the TSS Earnslaw, an old, coal-fired, twin-screw steamer, one of Queenstown's oldest attractions and known fondly by the locals as 'The Lady of the Lake'.

Another Queenstown favourite is the Skyline Gondola, which ascends to the top of Bob's Peak where a beautiful panorama awaits. There's plenty of action here too: a chair lift provides access to the top of the 800-metre-long luge, where punters race down on purpose-built carts; or you can plummet to earth from the Ledge Bungy, take off on a tandem parapente flight, or hike the Ben Lomond Track. Queenstown Combos provide a convenient and value-packed way to experience many of the adventure activities on offer in Queenstown and can be purchased at information centres or through Apex Car Rentals, Shotover Street, Queenstown. ■

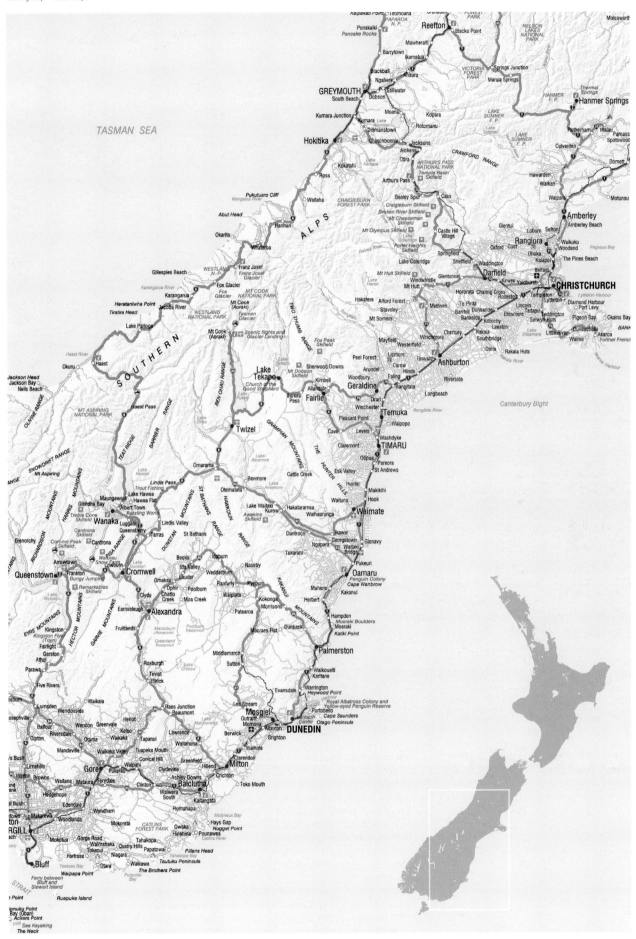

GOLFING

With more than 400 courses countrywide, New Zealand golf clubs offer beauty, diversity and value for money for the golfing enthusiast and with the highest number of golf courses per capita in the world there's a green here for everyone – literally!

Courses range from top of the line such as Kauri Cliffs in Northland to small rural golf clubs where greens are fenced off and stock graze the fairways, eliminating the need for mowing! At the Rotorua Golf Club in the Central North Island, the 16th hole features a steaming lake and bubbling mud pools; while Lake Taupo's Wairakei International Golf Course, reputed to have the most bunkers of any kiwi course, is home to NZ's most famous par five, the 14th, known as The Rogue and named after a geyser which used to erupt in a field nearby.

Scenery may not make the game, but it's not every day that you have the opportunity to play golf in the shadow of snow-capped mountains, surrounded by lush rolling countryside, brown velvety foothills and an aquamarine river so vivid it almost makes your eyes ache. Terrace Downs High Country Resort is nestled in the foothills of the Southern Alps, a 50-minute drive from Christchurch. Its championship 18-hole 72-par links style course

For those who would like to improve their game at Terrace Downs, a golf clinic is available upon demand. Qualified instructors offer both individual and group tuition. There's also a self-contained practice facility that includes a generous driving range, a short game area, practice bunkers and a choice of chipping and putting greens.

The clubhouse was inspired by mountain living and has the warmth and ambience of a high country homestead. It's superbly designed and constructed from rustic weathered cedar and local greywacke stone, and its enormous windows provide panoramic views of the course and the beautiful, snowcapped mountains beyond.

One of the really nice aspects of Terrace Downs is that everyone is welcome. There's plenty to entertain non-golfing partners and friends with a variety of other activities on offer. Mt Hutt Ski Field is also nearby making it a perfect après ski destination with two glorious spa pools set in front of massive bi-fold windows looking beyond to the mountains and – of course - nine holes of golf.

The food here is so good you won't want to leave. There's also a range of modern accommodation to choose from and, even better, every morning when you wake up, the river, the mountains and the renowned back nine will be there ready and waiting!

For further information view www.terracedowns.co.nz or from within NZ phone 0800 465 373.

sprawls over 200-odd acres, and while the walk may take a little longer than most, nobody ever complains! This stunning 6,440 metre long course with its nine lakes and 70 bunkers was laid out by Canadian golf architect Sid Puddicombe, while the back nine, largely designed by David Cox with some input from Fin Hobbs, is almost a signature feature.

"One of the best back nines we've played," wrote Tiger Woods' caddy, New Zealander Steve Williams. A sentiment echoed by many when they discover its challenging bunkers sited 20 to 40 metres short of the putting surface. Grassed, they slope to sand level so there's always room to swing, although your ball obviously won't go too far.

The most spectacular hole is found on the 16th where the tee hangs over the impressive Rakaia River Gorge and you look down upon fast flowing ice-blue water 200-metres below the course with the bulky range of Mt Hutt towering behind. The green is just a wedge or so away so you have to carry two ravines that drop all the way to the river through thick native bush. Your tee shot also has to carry a deep pot bunker short of the green and skirt another on the left. A short ball means an automatic reload but the faint hearted will soon discover a bail out area to the left. ▪

South Canterbury's flat plains, flanked by the dramatic peaks of the Southern Alps, stretch in a colourful patchwork of fields south to Timaru, the urban heart of the Central South Island. A lively, colourful town with a striking piazza overlooking Caroline Bay, Timaru has preserved much of its historical heritage in a collection of Edwardian and bluestone buildings, local museum treasures, and Maori rock art found in caves nearby. Further south, in Oamaru, a legacy in limestone awaits and the town's wonderful Victorian architecture – from banks to basilicas – is a rare sight to behold. Oamaru is home to a large colony of blue penguins and in Dunedin, where eco-tourism activities abound, visitors can get more than a glimpse of their yellow-eyed cousins.

We spend three days exploring the route from Christchurch to Dunedin. We take a historic train ride aboard the world's only Model T Ford Railcar, and sample classic slices of kiwiana before Bob begins training for a tramp. We explore Oamaru by foot; learn all about little blue penguins; and spy on 'Paul' as he squats atop a large pearly white egg.

CHRISTCHURCH TO DUNEDIN

DAY ONE
Christchurch to Timaru

"Well," says Bob, as we leave Christchurch airport where we've kicked off the day with an early morning visit to the Antarctic Centre, "those explorers are hardy types but I bet they love those Hägglunds!"

Rather taken with our simulated ride at the centre, he continues to relive the experience as we leave town and drive south on SH1 across the southern Canterbury plains to Ashburton and on to Temuka, a small town whose famous pottery has made its way into most NZ homes. At the Temuka Pottery Factory Shop we check out the stylish hand decorated terracotta pottery and enjoy an early lunch at its new, airy café.

Further south, in Timaru, we're greeted by a striking piazza overlooking Caroline Bay's popular sandy beach and fairgrounds. A flight of stairs cascade down to the bay but we continue along the main street past several fine local bluestone and Edwardian buildings to the information centre housed inside the historic Landing Service Building. Here we decide to spend the afternoon in Pleasant Point, a 15-minute drive inland, after exploring the highlights of Timaru.

Bob humours me with a walk through the Trevor Griffiths Rose Garden where we lose ourselves in the heady fragrance of 529 named old rose varieties, and then we explore Aigantighe Art Gallery's amazing exhibits of NZ art and sculpture.

At Pleasant Point I agree, somewhat reluctantly, to accompany Bob on a trip down memory lane aboard the world's only Model T Ford Railcar. It turns out to be great fun, but I tune out as Bob discusses the minute details of the restoration process with our friendly driver. We disembark at Keanes Crossing, where we're lead through a museum whose highlights include a Steam Locomotive AB699, a Steam Locomotive D16 (circa 1878), and NZ's only birdcage carriage, with pleated upholstery and a handcrafted kauri interior.

While Bob pores over beautifully restored engines and equipment, I wait it out in the Old Time Movie Theatre watching fascinating historical footage.

Finally I track Bob down. He's outside caressing the Model T.

"Well," I say, "I'm ready for a custard square."

"A what?" says Bob distractedly.

"Flaky pastry, creamy custard, lashings of icing," I say offhandedly. Vintage engine abruptly abandoned, Bob propels me back into the railcar.

At 'The Tearooms' in Denheath House, Pleasant Point, we order tea and custard squares.

This classic slice of kiwiana originated here and I feel truly patriotic tucking into my eight centimetre high tower of flaky golden pastry and fluffy melt-in-your-mouth filling, topped off with the creamiest icing.

"Oh my," says Bob, "heaven on a plate!"

Replete we visit modern-day blacksmith, Gareth James, at the Artisan Forge, then drive inland to Raincliff Reserve to admire Maori Rock Art on limestone overhangs. We return to Pleasant Point via Upper Waitohi and the memorial to pioneer aviator and inventor, Richard Pearse, who once made his home here. It's claimed that he flew using power before the Wright brothers, in 1903.

"Never!" exclaims Bob, triggering a debate that lasts all the way back to Timaru where we relax at a café in the piazza and watch the sunset over the mountains.

"Richard Pearse...well I don't know," concludes Bob as we finish our desserts, "But that Model T was something else!"

DAY TWO
Timaru to Oamaru

I awake to find Bob gone. He returns a little later looking sweaty but decidedly pleased and announces that he's been 'jogging' at Caroline Bay.

"I'm thinking about hiking the Kepler Track," he says, much to my amazement, "but I've only got a couple of weeks or so to get fit!"

Privately I have my doubts about the wisdom of a strenuous three to four day tramp, but who am I to judge? "Great goal," I say encouragingly, as we pack our bags and leave for Oamaru. En route we make a detour to Waimate, the strawberry capital of the south, where large brush wallabies roam in Hunters Hills behind town. We enjoy coffee and berry muffins at Wildberry Café then, with the delicious aroma of freshly baked wallaby pies wafting on the breeze, pop into Enkledoovery Korna where Bob cuddles a tame wallaby and poses for a photo.

"Aren't wallabies Australian natives?" he asks, as we drive away. I explain how they - along with the pesky possum - were unwittingly introduced to NZ.

A short time later we arrive in Oamaru, which has the largest collection of protected heritage buildings in NZ. Crafted from a creamy-textured local limestone known as Oamaru Stone, these gorgeous Victorian buildings with their huge columns and extensive ornamentation were designed by the finest architects of their time.

We head straight for the Harbour and Tyne Historical Precinct, reputed to be the only intact Victorian harbour in NZ, where there's a curved wooden wharf. We watch craftsmen sculpt Oamaru stone, then drop in to sample a cheese platter at Whitestone Cheese before (in the interests of Bob's fitness regime) setting off on a self-guided walking tour of the town.

We hike up the hill to the late nineteenth century St Patrick's Basilica, with its coffered ren-aissance ceiling and an impressive dome over the sanctuary, then continue on to 56 Eden St where Janet Frame lived for 14 years. A number of extracts from her earlier manuscripts can be seen in Oamaru. We admire the magnificent trees and flower beds in the 1876 gardens,

Christchurch to Dunedin:
Attractions and Activities

Temuka Homeware: www.temukahomeware.co.nz
Aigantighe Gallery: Timaru
Pleasant Pt Railway: www.timaru.com/railway/
Artisan Forge: www.iron.co.nz
Maori Rock Art: Timaru
Enkledoovery Korna: Waimate
Oamaru Blue Penguin Colony: www.penguins.co.nz
Bushy Penguin Colony: Oamaru
Moeraki Boulders: Moeraki
Penguin Place: www.penguin-place.co.nz

Christchurch to Dunedin:
Cafés and Eateries

Temuka Homeware Factory Shop: Vine St, SH1, Temuka
The Tearooms: Denheath House, Pleasant Pt
Café Piazza: 64 The Bay Hill, Timaru
Wildberry Café: Waimate
Whitestone Cheese: 3 Torridge St, Oamaru
Criterion Hotel: The Old Quarter, Oamaru
Fleur's Place: The Old Jetty, Moeraki

> We watch in the fading light as a hundred or so penguins ride in on the waves, awkwardly right themselves, then waddle up the stony beach

and relax at the Italian marble fountain. A stroll along the train track takes us back to Tees Street, home of St Luke's Anglican Church (1866), the former Post Office building (1883), the North Otago Museum (1882) and the old Courthouse built in 1882-3.

"I'm ready for a beer," Bob declares, so we relax over a cold Speights in the Criterion Hotel's olde-worlde bar and dine upon their specialty pies – sausage meat with fillings of cheese, tomato or mushroom. Earlier in the day we booked a blue penguin tour, so after dinner we follow the waterfront past shag-smothered piers and the Red Sheds' craft displays to the Oamaru Blue Penguin Colony. The evening begins with a behind-the-scenes view and history of the colony, then we watch in the fading light as a hundred or so birds ride in on the waves, awkwardly right themselves, then waddle up the stony beach. At the top they stop to preen, then with an unconcerned air continue their ungainly gait past where we're seated and return to their cliff-side homes. "Let's go spot their yellow-eyed cousins tomorrow at sunrise," says Bob, elated, "I'll walk and you can follow me in the car."

DAY THREE
Oamaru to Dunedin

Next morning, true to his word, there's no sign of Bob except a note on the table. I load our bags and drive to the top of a steep hill where I spot Bob doing stretching exercises.

I pull up alongside and he hops in gratefully.

A little further along is the Bushy Beach Penguin Colony, where we huddle together in the Dept. of Conservation hide with cameras at the ready.

Suddenly a penguin pops out of the grassy bank above the beach and lands on the sand. Further up the beach another follows suit, and they both waddle to the sea in unison.

"Their eyes are extraordinary," says Bob, zooming in, "but I'd like to see them closer."

When no other penguins appear, we walk back to the car and head south towards Dunedin. Thirty-five minutes later we arrive in the tiny fishing village of Moeraki and park by the jetty, outside a popular café called Fleur's Place. We set off briskly along the beach to the Moeraki Boulders, accompanied en route by a mischievous pod of common dolphins.

After marvelling at the perfect roundness of the large boulders, we head back to Fleur's where we have some deliciously fresh scallops and Thai fish cakes before driving south along picturesque Katiki Beach and on through Palmerston, which gleams with fresh paint.

As the sun dips low in the sky and the landscape changes to ranges and deep forested valleys, we descend into Dunedin. A wealth of eco-activities await but our first port of call is Penguin Place, where Howard McGrouther leads us through an intricate network of burrows in the dunes to large cavern-like hides. Bob clicks off round after round as a penguin known as 'Paul' carefully shuffles his white belly over a huge pearly egg until it disappears from view.

"Unforgettable," Bob whispers. "It's absolutely unforgettable." ∎

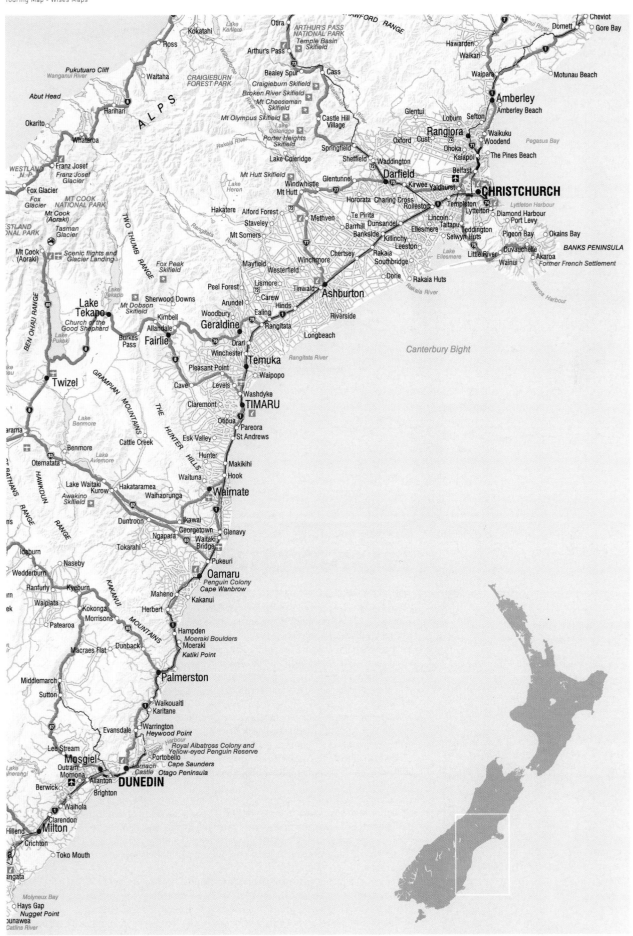

DUNEDIN ECOLOGY

When world-renowned ecologist Sir David Bellamy visited Dunedin in the year 2000 he was impressed by what he saw. "In my opinion the Otago Peninsula is the finest example of eco-tourism in the world," he said.

It's a claim that few would challenge, as there are not too many cities around the globe that boast such a diverse range of wildlife all within easy reach of the city. Dunedin's Otago Peninsula offers it all: from frolicking seal pups and lazy sea lions, to thriving populations of rare yellow eyed penguin and the only accessible mainland colony of Northern Royal Albatross in the world.

And it's this unique phenomenon, seen at the Royal Albatross Centre located on Taiaroa Head on the tip of the peninsula, which remains the highlight for most visitors to the city. The centre controls visitor numbers and operates under strict Dept. of Conservation ruling.

For a small entry fee, eco-guides lead groups up to the observatory where there's a good view of these giant birds either sitting upon their eggs or soaring in the sky above like gigantic hang gliders.

There are 24 species of albatross and the Northern Royal Albatross is the largest of them all with a wing span of up to three metres. These allow them to use the wind current to its best advantage and spend up to a year at a time at sea, sleeping and feeding on the water. Around eighty percent of a Northern Royal Albatross's life is spent at sea and they can glide for days at a time, averaging an incredible 500 km per day as they circumnavigate the southern oceans.

The birds usually choose to nest on inaccessible offshore islands, but in 1914 the first Northern Royal Albatross began to land at Taiaroa Head. In 1920 an egg was discovered and since then the colony has slowly grown and now boasts around 100 resident birds.

At Taiaroa Head the parent birds, who share incubation duty, sometimes wait for up to five days for their mate to return and relieve them. After 11 weeks the albatross chick hatches

and its parents will continue to care for it for another nine months, before they leave to spend a year at sea. The juvenile, who has never flown or fed itself before, waits on the high cliffs of Taiaroa for a strong wind then launches itself into the air, and - like its parents – doesn't return until the following year.

In the meantime locals anxiously await their return and when the first albatross arrives back at the colony, church bells peal for one hour to let the city know that the birds have arrived home safely.

On the rocks below the heads, NZ fur seals and sea lions laze in the sun. They can be viewed aboard a scenic boat ride with Monarch Wildlife Cruises or on kayak tours. Seal pups are best seen at Nature's Wonders where visitors can board an all-terrain Argo for a ride across a private farm to watch baby seals frolic in naturally formed rock pools.

Other local marine life can be viewed at the Marine Studies Centre and Aquarium in Portobello, the Marine Science Department of Otago University, where extensive studies are underway on NZ seaweed. The aquarium features many species of fish and a series of 'touchpools' – rock pools teeming with colourful sea creatures for kids to explore. Here you can also feed hungry pigfish, shake hands with an octopus or peek inside a shark's egg.

The Otago Peninsula's colonies of Yellow Eyed Penguins can be viewed from a number of hides provided by DOC along the coastline and the best time to spot a penguin waddling to shore is just after sunrise and an hour before sunset.

At Howard McGrouther's Penguin Place, where humans are caged and wildlife roams free, these rare penguins can be seen - especially during the breeding season - at most times of the day! This Yellow-Eyed Penguin Conservation Reserve is a private effort to save one of the world's most endangered penguins from extinction.

When the penguins began to settle on the McGrouther's farm, Howard dug an intricate network of burrows by hand so he wouldn't disturb the wildlife or scar the landscape. The burrows travel through the dunes for 400 metres to hides where visitors can peer through narrow gaps and see the penguins squatting over huge pearly-white eggs.

The yellow-eyed penguins lay their eggs in the second half of September and, like the Royal Northern Albatross, both parents share the incubation period. The chicks hatch in Novem-

ber and then in mid-February they leave for the sea where they spend six weeks to six months at large before returning to the colony.

Penguin Place has a penguin hospital on site and a scientist is employed to help monitor their progress. Whilst most penguins prefer to live under the cover of bush – and many at Penguin Place do – some choose to nest out in the open. Protection is important for young chicks so in the interests of safety, Howard places an A-frame hut over the top of their nests. "They pick their nesting spot, I just provide them with a bit of shelter," he says.

A couple of sheep roam between the nests to keep the grass short. This in turn keeps the mouse population down and their predators, the stoats and ferrets away. "Ecology is like a giant jigsaw puzzle," says Howard, "Each piece is required to make up the whole picture."

Visitors can self-drive to the Otago Peninsula to explore its many attractions or alternatively arrange a tour through the Dunedin Visitor Centre. ■

The Southern Scenic Route, which curves around the southern coast of the South Island from Dunedin through the Catlins to Invercargill, then on up SH95 to Te Anau, provides a range of dramatic scenery. From rocky islets, sparkling waterfalls, high headlands, thunderous surf, quaint fishing villages, and dense native forests to snowcapped mountains and mirrored lakes the landscape provides eye candy for all tastes. We spend three days travelling this scenic route and complete several short walks along the way. We visit spectacular Purakaunui Falls, dine on Bluff oysters, touch Jurassic tuatara, and rescue cast sheep on our farm stay at Mt Prospect station.

Bob also learns to free dive and prepare paua ready for the BBQ, stalks deer with a local hunter at night, and discovers that thanks to a bit of kiwi ingenuity, anyone can enjoy a day's hiking on a Great Walk, no matter how fit they are!

DUNEDIN
TO TE ANAU

DAY ONE
Dunedin to Curio Bay

After embracing kiwi culture and attending a spirited rugby game between the Canterbury and Otago at Carisbrook Stadium the previous evening, Bob and I leave town on the Southern Scenic Route bound for Curio Bay.

We travel alongside magnificent beaches en route to Taieri Mouth where fishing boats line the river, before climbing high into the hills and descending to Lake Waihola. Following a quiet cup of thermos tea on its peaceful shores, we continue on through Milton and Balclutha and then turn off for the Catlins, following the well signposted Southern Scenic Route.

Our first stop, shortly after the seaside village of Kaka Point, is at Nugget Point where we walk a narrow and windswept trail to the lighthouse. It's perched upon a high, narrow spur of land that juts into the ocean, with a steep drop to the rocks below where elephant seals, sea lions and fur seals and a colony of gannets make their home. The nuggets, a series of rounded rock islets, protrude from the ocean like a random scattering of raisins.

"Impressive," says Bob, leaning into the keen wind as we admire the view before continuing on to Owaka via Cannibal Bay, the traditional homeland of adult bull sea lions who return here after breeding. Finding the beach deserted, we drive to an old-fashioned kiwi tearoom on the main street of Owaka and tuck into egg mayonnaise sandwiches.

We make a stop at Catlins Adventures, which provides a tourist information service and offers horse riding, deep sea charter fishing, fly fishing and hunting excursions, then pay a visit to Owaka's Mushroom Man, Jason Skinley, who crafts brightly painted wooden toadstools in a shed attached to his home. I purchase several for my garden and we drive on to the renowned Purakaunui Falls where a ten-minute walk leads us through mixed podocarp and beech forest to a beautiful waterfall tumbling over three or more ledges.

At nearby Purakaunui Bay, with its high dramatic cliffs that featured in the movie, The Lion, the Witch and the Wardrobe, a group of Friesian cows follow us onto the beach.

Bob gasps as they begin to munch on stringy kelp. "It's edible and makes great seaweed chips," I reassure him, laughing as his face lights up at the thought of a new culinary delight.

We continue on to Papatowai, a sleepy seaside town with a small store and a curiosity shop/museum housed in an old bus, and on up to the Florence Hill Lookout which offers an amazing view of Tautuku Beach, smothered with jungle-like native forest right down to the shore. We hop out for a barefoot paddle then drive to Lake Wilkie, nestled amongst broad-leaved flowering trees and ancient podocarps.

It's a 30-minute return hike to the lake but we choose the five minute walk to a viewing platform where we're surrounded by flittering fantails.

Back in the car we drive past the entrance for the Cathedral Caves (a 20-minute hike across private farmland and only accessible at low tide), and on through rolling hills framed by the dense rainforest of the Catlins Forest Park. In Niagara we stop at the Niagara Falls Café and Gallery housed in an old renovated school and enjoy huge slabs of homemade banana cake washed down with gallons of tea. We peruse the gifts and local arts in the gallery then take a short walk to the Niagara Falls, named by a surveyor with a rich sense of humour. We gaze at the trickle of water splashing over the rocks. "Nothing like a good imagination!" Bob observes with a smile.

In nearby Waikawa we take some time to explore the museum's whaling, sawmilling and goldmining displays.

At 4 pm we decide to check into Curio Bay Boutique Accommodation at Porpoise Bay. Our friendly hosts, Nick and Dani Stratford, invite us to share their evening meal, but first it must be gathered from the bay. Bob pulls on his swimming trunks and joins Nick to free-dive for paua, while I walk along the beach to Curio Bay where a 180-million-year-old fossilised forest lies embedded in the rocks. As the light begins to fade I retreat to a viewing platform and watch as a pair of yellow-eyed penguins (hoiho) waddle up the rocky shore, stop to preen, then continue their ungainly gait to their nests.

Back at the lodge Nick is teaching Bob how to prepare paua, carefully cutting each from its shell and wrapping it in a cloth. Then it's tenderised with several good thumps from an axe by Bob (who takes his axe-wielding duties seriously) and soon they're sizzling on the BBQ. Nick gives them one minute a side and we devour them hot off the grill.

"Mouthwatering," declares Bob, smacking his lips, "let's get some more for breakfast!"

DAY TWO
Curio Bay to Riverton

True to his word Bob is out back pounding the paua as dawn breaks, and we enjoy a fresh seafood breakfast before bidding Nick and Dani farewell.

We make a stop so Bob can visit the fossilised forest, then drive to Slope Point, the southern-most tip of the South Island. It's a windy, isolated place where macrocarpa trees form thick shelterbelts and grow almost horizontally in a bid to escape the salt-laden wind.

From here it's a short drive to the lighthouse at Waipapa Point where, much to our surprise, we share the car park with a group of basking sea lions. Carefully we pick our way across to the lighthouse and scour the coast for NZ fur seals and - a rarer visitor - the four-ton elephant seal. A memorial plaque reminds us, on a more sobering note, that 131 people lost their lives here in 1881when the SS Tararua hit the reef.

We drive on to Fortrose at the mouth of the Mataura River and then leave the Catlins behind, travelling through farmland to Invercargill and on to Bluff. Here we enjoy a delicious lunch of fresh Bluff oysters, then follow a spiral walkway to a lookout point providing excellent views of

Dunedin to Te Anau:
Attractions and Activities

Nugget Point: Owaka
Catlins Adventures: www.catlinsadventures.co.nz
Purakaunui Falls: Owaka
Waikawa Museum: Waikawa
Southland Museum: www.southlandmuseum.co.nz
Something Special Gallery: www.somethingspecial.co.nz
Riverton Arts Centre: Riverton
Fossilised Forest: Curio Bay
Waipapa Point: Catlins
Maritime Museum: www.bluff.co.nz/museum.html

Dunedin to Te Anau:
Cafés and Eateries

Lumber Jack Café: 3 Saunders St, Owaka
Niagara Falls Café & Gallery: Niagara Falls, Waikawa
Superior Oysters Ltd: 136 Dee St, Invercargill
Anchorage Café: 86 Gore St, Bluff
Beachhouse Café: 126 Rocks Hwy, Riverton
Country Nostalgia: 108 Palmerston St, Riverton
Miles Better Pies: Milford Rd, Te Anau

> " We choose the five minute walk to a viewing platform where we're surrounded by flittering fantails "

Bluff harbour and the city beyond. Our next port of call is the Southland Museum and Art Gallery in Invercargill, for its 'live' tuatara display. Lindsay Hazley, the world's leading tuatara expert, set up the display 15 years ago and here he breeds the endangered Brother's Island tuatara, and the rare "common" tuatara. Around 40 tuatara are on display and Lindsay relates the history and habits of these unique living dinosaurs, then shows us a baby common tuatara and a pregnant mother whose reptilian skin is cold to the touch.

It's all so riveting that it's hard to leave, but eventually we tear ourselves away and drive to the quaint fishing village of Riverton, where we check into the Riverton Rock Guesthouse. After a hot cuppa with our host, Francis Michels, and a couple of her friends – Jill Nicholls from Something Special Gallery across the road and local hunter Rob Ashworth – Bob (much to his delight) is invited to go deer stalking and heads off with Rob, while I pop across the road with Jill to see her collection. There's a fine range of works on display by a select group of NZ artists, weavers, woodturners, sculptors and other craftspeople. Each piece is hand picked by Jill and the gallery really

is, as its name suggests, something rather special!

Later, after a delicious meal at the Beachhouse Café and a hot chocolate with Francis, I retire to the Scarlet room, and wallow in its deep Victorian bath before slipping into a deep sleep.

DAY THREE
Riverton to Te Anau

In the morning I awake early and take a brisk walk up the main street to admire Riverton's wealth of heritage buildings. When I return, Bob's nursing a strong cup of coffee but he perks up when he sees me.

"We got back at 3 am...45 kilos...shot in the heart.." he gabbles excitedly as we load our gear into the boot. He's still raving about the hunt as we drive past Colac Bay.

"It was unbelievable, he gutted the deer then wore it like a backpack to cart it out!" he says.

"Oh well they're hardy these southern men," I reply, pointing out Cosy Nook, a tiny fishing village with a handful of cribs (holiday homes). Bob waves to some fishermen on a boat heading out into a high sea from the sheltered, rocky bay. We continue on to McCracken's Rest with its picture-postcard views of Te Wae Wae Bay and Solander Island, then we leave the coast and drive inland through Tuatapere to Clifden. Here we stop to admire its historic suspension bridge and then drive on, under the watchful gaze of the Takitimu Mountain Range, to Lake Manapouri, which is surrounded by the snowcapped Hunter Mountains, Turret Range, and Cathedral and Jackson Peaks.

Bob clicks off a few rounds with his camera and then we continue on to Te Anau for a late lunch of gourmet venison pies from 'Miles better Pies', eaten seated upon a picnic table on the lakeshore.

"There's the Kepler Mountains," I point out as Bob greedily wolfs down a second pie, "and that's Mt Luxmoore, the highest point on the Kepler Track."

"Looks pretty tough," says Bob, chewing thoughtfully and carefully

avoiding eye contact, clearly having decided that his aim of experiencing a Great Walk in NZ may not become a reality.

"Don't worry," I say, gathering our gear together, "let's get some more information."

We drive to the Dept. of Conservation office where we watch a video about the track and pick up a brochure. Both recommend a good level of fitness and Bob looks decidedly uncomfortable.

Sensing the need for a change of scenery I suggest we check into our farmstay at Mt Prospect early. "You're going to love it," I tell Bob, trying to distract him as we head out to the isolated station.

When we pull up outside the huge farmhouse at Mt Prospect Station we're greeted by our friendly hosts, Joan and Ross Cockburn, who usher us inside, show us to our rooms, then invite us to join them for afternoon tea. After freshening up I return to the lounge where Bob is regaling Ross with all the highlights of our circumnavigation of NZ. Ruby the cat sits on his lap.

After tea we pile into a four wheel drive for a tour of the farm. "We're shearing this week," says Ross, " so there could be a few cast about."

I smile because I know Bob will have no idea what he means and as Ross begins to tell us more about his family's nine thousand-acre merino sheep and cattle farm, he suddenly interrupts.

"Look," he cries, pointing at a sheep pedalling its hooves in the air,

"it's having a seizure!"

"Good spotting," says Ross. "But it's okay, it happens just before they're shorn as they're a bit top heavy."

We jump out and wander over to the helpless sheep, which quickly rights itself after an almighty shove from Ross and Bob.

"Right," says Ross, nodding at Mt Prospect after it's sorted, "let's head on up the hill." We drive up a steep track to the summit where we're offered a stunning 360-degree view of the surrounding countryside, snowcapped mountains, the full spread of Lake Te Anau and Lake Manapouri in the distance.

"Wow," says Bob his arms outstretched, "it's like being in a plane."

We stand for a time admiring the lakes and mountain ranges in the setting sun, then Ross names each mountain, ending with Mt Luxmoore. "More magic views from across there," he says.

"I know," says Bob forlornly, "I hoped to hike the Kepler, but I'm too unfit."

"No worries," says Ross taking in Bob's rather ample frame, "you can fly in to Luxmoore Hut – from there it's just a short hike to the top – then walk downhill to Brod Bay and water taxi out."

"Really?" asks Bob, turning to me, his face lighting up.

"Absolutely," says Ross firmly, "we'll sort it out later, but now it's time for some of Joan's roast lamb." ■

Stewart Island, or Rakiura (glowing skies) as it is known to the Maori, is one of NZ's least explored eco-tourism destinations. Granite-based with high rocky outcrops it offers a mix of deep clear bays, white sandy beaches and towering emerald-green rainforest.

An ecological wonderland, three-quarters of the island is part of the Rakiura National Park. As the fourth largest park in NZ, it boasts some 157,000 hectares which teem with wildlife. The island is a paradise for trampers and nature lovers, offering many visitors the rare privilege of an unexpected rendezvous with a kiwi.

There are around 20,000 Stewart Island kiwi on the island. One of the larger species of this flightless bird, they are often seen foraging in the forest or hunting for sand hoppers on the beach. For those who do not come across one on their travels, kiwi-spotting night tours are available. Places are limited so it's best to book in advance.

Stewart Island is also popular with birdwatchers because it has the largest and most diverse bird population in NZ, from the vividly feathered kaka and parakeet to the tui and bellbird with their melodic calls. Seabirds abound: there are several species of albatross and five types of penguin, including the tiny blue penguin and the rare yellow-eyed penguin – to name just a few! Ulva Island, a short boat ride from Stewart Island, is a pest-free open sanctuary where visitors can view and learn about many species that don't thrive well on the mainland islands due to pests such as stoats, rats, and feral cats. The Stewart Island robin, South Island saddleback and the mohua (or yellowhead) are some of the rare birds likely to be encountered. The weka – often mistaken for kiwi – is prolific and these friendly birds usually provide a welcome committee. Day trips to Ulva Island can be organised at the Visitors' Centre in Oban.

STEWART ISLAND

Stewart Island's DOC Visitors' Centre provides information on the island's network of hiking trails. There's a number of short hikes which range from 15 minutes to seven hours as well as several longer tramps which journey across the island through ancient podocarp forests of rimu, miro, southern kamahi and a dense carpet of ferns. The 36-kilometre Rakiura Track is extremely popular. It's one of NZ's Great Walks and can be covered in three days. It crosses the sheltered shores of Paterson Inlet and features historical sites and a mix of forest and open coast.

The North West Circuit is a challenging 125-kilometre, ten-day hike for the hardier tramper and tackles some of the island's most rugged terrain, while the Southern Circuit (which can be added to the North West Circuit to create a complete Stewart Island experience) takes six to nine days to complete. Comfortable huts on all the tracks provide toilets, running water, wood stoves and mattresses.

For underwater explorers there's abundant marine life to be discovered amongst the tall bladder kelp, a 70-foot long kelp unique to the island. It can be explored on a snorkelling or diving trip, while chartered boat tours, deep sea fishing and sea kayak trips allow you to soak up the island's sights by sea. Fishing is excellent and delicious blue cod can be caught from the rocks.

The island's original Maori name: Te Punga O Te Waka a Maui (the anchor stone of Maui's Canoe) refers to the part played in the legend of Maui and his crew, who from their canoe (the South Island) caught a great fish (the North Island). The island's English name came courtesy of First Officer William Stewart, who charted the southern coast aboard the Pegasus in 1809.
Today Stewart Island's 400 or so inhabitants (many descended directly from Maori and European settlers) mostly live in or around Oban, the island's only town. The pub provides a social centre and one of several dining options available to the visitor. As there are no banks on Stewart Island it pays to bring some cash, but most businesses accept EFTPOS or credit card.

For day trippers, bus tours cover most of the island's 20-kilometres of road in an hour or so and give an excellent introduction to its history. Longer bus tours include bush walks with experienced naturalists.

Stewart Island can be reached by a daily scheduled ferry service from Bluff which takes around an hour, or a 20-minute flight from Invercargill airport. ■

Some of NZ's wildest and most dramatic scenery can be found in Fiordland, from waterfalls that tumble through dense forests of beech into deep ice carved fiords, to shimmering lakes and small towns cradled amongst magnificent mountains. Fiordland has 14 fiords which are carved through steep mountain ranges and span some 215 kilometres of coastline, and of these Doubtful and Milford Sound are the most accessible to the visitor. Fiordland also offers many hiking tracks from the popular Milford Track to the lesser-known Kepler Track, Routeburn and Hollyford, as well as numerous short walks. We take four days to explore Fiordland's pristine wilderness. Bob fulfills his wish to hike on the Kepler Track, we take a cruise on Milford Sound, visit the Te Anau Glowworm Caves, discover tranquil Doubtful Sound aboard the Fiordland Navigator and Bob tries his hand at sheep shearing!

FIORDLAND AND **MILFORD SOUND**

DAY ONE
Kepler Track

"Hi ho, hi ho, la-la la-la la," I hear Bob yodel as we slowly hike the trail which leads from Luxmoore Hut to the summit of Mt Prospect. It's an ascent of around 400 metres but there's no rush as we have all day.

At 11am, after an incredibly scenic helicopter ride over Fiordland's snowcapped peaks, lakes, rivers and fiords, we were dropped at Luxmoore Hut on the Kepler Track, well above the tree line. Bob sets our pace and he's doing well but as we reach the ridge below the summit of Mt Luxmoore (1472 metres) he's ready for a break.

"I'm glad we're day hiking," he says, nodding his head at an athletic-looking pair hiking past with bursting backpacks, full of equipment and food. We've also come well equipped, but on a smaller scale, with waterproof clothing, plenty of water, food and high energy snacks in our daypacks. The weather may be near perfect, but conditions can suddenly change in the mountains.

Bob bites a snack bar and within moments we have company. A cheeky kea emerges from behind a shaggy snow tussock. "Don't feed it," I warn, as Bob breaks off a piece.

Instead he pops it into his mouth and takes a photo, then we continue on a sidetrack to the summit of Mt Luxmoore, arriving breathlessly at the top 15 minutes later.

"Wow," marvels Bob, "look at that view!"

Lake Te Anau spreads before us and we have panoramic 360-degree views of the South Arm, Te Anau Basin, Takitimu Mountains, Jackson Peaks and the Snowden and Earl mountains.

"There's Mt Prospect," says Bob, pointing across the lake to a peak rising above the station where we're staying for the duration of our Fiordland experience.

We find a sheltered nook and relax in the sun absorbing the peace and watching skylarks suspended in the air above wide open tussock slopes below. We lunch on cheese and crackers then, after taking photos of mountain daisies, begin our descent to Brod Bay.

Soon after Luxmoore Hut we hit the stunted bushline where bonsai-like silver beech trees dominate, becoming thicker and taller as we descend, then grudgingly make space for silver and red beech, kamahi, miro and rimu wearing garlands of mosses, and perching plants. We stop for a breather at the limestone bluffs, then continue on through a forest alive with the song of bellbirds. Fantails, tomtits and grey warblers flutter in the bushes nearby.

At last we emerge at Brod Bay and wait for our water taxi to Te Anau. "We could walk," says Bob doubtfully, looking at his watch.

"No, it's booked," I say, "Here it comes."

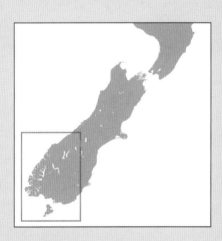

We watch as the speedboat crosses the lake and pulls alongside. "Great day for it!" says the skipper, as we climb gratefully aboard.

Back in Te Anau I glance at Bob, who looks tired but happy. "What now?" I ask.

"A hot shower, clean clothes, feet up by the fire and a glass of Pinot followed by some of Joan's smoked salmon," says Bob.

"She's making her rolled pavlova tonight," I suddenly recall.

"That's right," says Bob smiling, well pleased with his day's hiking. "I think that we've earned it!"

DAY TWO
Milford Sound

The sounds of a shearing gang setting up comes from the shed as we pass by bound for Milford Sound. We've a 115km journey ahead of us through some of NZ's most scenic countryside yet the weather, which looked so promising yesterday, has packed in.

"What a shame," cries Bob as we drive through the Eglinton Valley. After some 55 kilometres we stop at the Mirror Lakes, but there's no reflections of mountains today.

Fortunately Bob picked up a copy of the "Road to Milford Sound", a 60-minute commentary and he slips the disc into our trusty rental car's CD player. It's extremely informative and takes our mind off the weather.

"Stop," yells Bob suddenly as we pass a sign: "Latitude 45 Degrees South". He insists on having his photo taken, even though it's pouring with rain. Soaked, and thankful for our vehicle's heating, we continue on past Cascade Creek, Lake Gunn and Lake Fergus to the Kaka Creek Lookout overlooking the Hollyford Valley.

A kea joins us as we wait hopefully for the view, much of which is obscured by thick clouds. Occasionally we catch provocative glimpses of what lies behind, before the weather closes in again.

We continue on, passing through an active avalanche area where signs warn us that snow chains are mandatory from May to September.

Suddenly, without warning, we shoot through low cloud into the Homer Tunnel and begin a sharp descent through the heart of a mountain. More low cloud follows and then we arrive at Milford Sound village. After a hot meal at the café, we don raincoats and walk to the harbour to board a Red Boat for our cruise of the Milford Sound.

"Two out of every three days it rains at Milford Sound," says our guide, Nathan. "But the good news is that Milford Sound's spectacular in any weather!"

The rain eases, so Bob and I climb up to the viewing platform where we gain complete panoramic views of the sound's high dramatic headlands. Misty clouds cling to peaks and hollows adding an eerie, mystical air, and dozens of magnificent waterfalls tumble into a deep, teal-green sea.

We cruise past a cloud-swathed Mitre Peak, taking in Copper Point's metallic deposits and Fairy Falls before we reach Dale Point at the entrance of the fiord. Here we turn around and make our way via Seal Rock, complete with a pair of seals, to the magnificent Stirling Falls, which plummet some 155 metres and are at their most spectacular after such heavy rain.

Fiordland:
Attractions and Activities

Kepler Track: search www.doc.govt.nz
Fiordland Helicopters: www.fiordlandhelicopters.co.nz
Kepler Water Taxi: Te Anau
Mt Prospect Station: www.lodgings.co.nz/prospect.html
Milford Sound Cruise: www.realjourneys.co.nz
Kayak Milford: www.kayakmilford.co.nz
Te Anau Glowworm Caves: www.realjourneys.co.nz
Ata Whenua: www.fiordlandcinema.co.nz
Te Anau Wildlife Centre: Te Anau
Doubtful Sound Cruise: www.realjourneys.co.nz

Fiordland:
Cafés and Eateries

Sandfly Café: 9 The Lane, Te Anau
Redcliff Café: 12 Mokonui St, Te Anau
Beehive Café: 68 Cathedral Dr, Manapouri
Blue Duck Café: Milford Sound
Josswood: Te Anau-Mossburn Hwy, Te Anau
Pop Inn Café: 92 Te Anau Tce, Te Anau
The Olive Tree Café: 52 Town Centre, Te Anau

> Misty clouds cling to peaks and hollows adding an eerie, mystical air, and dozens of magnificent waterfalls tumble into a deep, teal-green sea

"Amazing," says Bob shooting photo after photo, "it's beautiful!"

We pass by the underwater observatory in Harrison Cove, which is framed by snowcapped Mt Pembroke with its 27 metre long remnant of a glacier that once carved its way through the fiord. Finally, on our return to the wharf at Freshwater Basin, we pass the gushing Lady Bowen Falls, an incredible 161-metre drop from a hanging valley.

"Well," says Bob, as we disembark, and begin the return drive to Mt Prospect Station, "I can't think of anywhere else in the world that looks so stunning in the rain!"

DAY THREE
Te Anau

We enjoy a slow start, relaxing over a hearty farm breakfast washed down with aromatic, freshly brewed coffee. Bob reflects that after such a long time on the road it's refreshing to stay in the same place for several days in a row.

Grant, our hosts' son, who lives in a cottage nearby with his wife

Rachel and their two-year-old daughter Ellie, joins us for his morning coffee. He says he grew up on the farm and after a career in the city for several years, was drawn back to station life. Like many growing up on isolated high country stations, he attended boarding school for much of his schooling.

Bob follows him over to the noisy, organised chaos of the shearing sheds to learn about the process, while I join Joan in the kitchen, and write down her pavlova recipe. "The secret is fifteen minutes at 180 degrees Celsius before you roll it," she confides.

An hour later Bob returns from the shearing shed having had an impromptu lesson. "It's a lot harder than it looks," he tells me.

We head into town where our first port of call is the Te Anau Wildlife Centre to see its wonderful variety of native birds. After a light lunch at a local café we board a Real Journeys scenic cruise to the Te Anau Glowworm Caves. We disembark at the wharf where beech trees grow down to the waterline and follow our guide, Heath Hollows, to Cavern House to watch an audiovisual presentation on how the caves were formed.

Heath leads us underground to explore a mysterious world of strange rock formations, fossils and gushing waterfalls, before ushering us aboard a small boat to float beneath a myriad of starry glowworms.

After a short bush walk we return to Cavern House and look through its museum before cruising back to Te Anau, where Bob hunts for souvenirs at its small shopping centre.

Then we relax with a glass of wine at Te Anau's ultra-modern cinema and sit back to enjoy Ata Whenua, a 32-minute scenic journey produced by local helicopter pilot, Kim Hollows. It gives a breathtaking taste of the Fiordland World Heritage Wilderness that most visitors would otherwise never see, and as we sit down for dinner at Te Anau's acclaimed Redcliff Café, Bob's still raving about it.

"It's a visual feast!" he tells our waitress, and then he turns to me. "I hope the weather improves tomorrow," he says, "I want to see as much as we can."

DAY FOUR
Doubtful Sound

Bob's wish is granted as the day dawns bright and clear. "It will be wonderful," Joan promises us as we leave Mt Prospect Station, stopping first to watch as Ross and his dogs – Spark, Flirt, Joe and Oak – skillfully round up shorn sheep and move them to a neighbouring paddock.

Meanwhile Grant's checking the 'mothering on' pens. Last night he said that he'd skinned a dead lamb, tied its coat onto an orphan and put it in with the dead lamb's mother. "Once it has a drink and the milk goes through, it'll smell just like its own lamb," he said.

As we drive by he gives us thumbs up and waves a lamb's skin in the air - the adoption process is successful!

We drive to Pearl Harbour at Lake Manapouri where we board a boat and travel up the scenic West Arm of the lake. Our skipper, Terry, points out mountains en route and says that like Loch Ness in Scotland, Manapouri has a monster, "except ours is bigger and much better looking!" she jokes.

We disembark at the Real Journeys Visitor Centre which provides detailed information on Lake Manapouri and Doubtful Sound as well as clean facilities. From the Centre, we board a bus with Alex Mackay, our guide for the day, at the wheel and follow a private road through native bush to a lookout point at the top of the Wilmot Pass.

The view of Doubtful Sound from the lookout is staggering. Alex tells us that according to Maori legend the fiords of this region were not created by glaciers, but by Tu Te Raki Whanoa, a god-like figure who cut them with a magical adze. When it came to Doubtful Sound he sought assistance from four young sea gods who carved out its sheltered arms.

Down on the dock we have another surprise in store: the catamaran Commander Peak is in for a service so our small group gets the chance to cruise aboard the luxurious overnight vessel, the magnificent Fiordland Navigator.

"I'm feeling pretty special," says Bob, as we explore this huge ship and find ourselves a perfect possie on its huge upper forward deck. Here we enjoy a yummy pre-ordered lunch surrounded by ever changing 360-degree views. There are waterfalls aplenty, dropping from rocky ledges and splashing through dense native bush to where seals bask on rocks in the sun. We travel up to the entrance of Doubtful Sound – which we discover is not actually a sound at all, but a fiord with a case of mistaken identity – and peek into Crooked Arm and Hall Arm where the mountains are perfectly reflected upon the still waters.

Bob and I are transfixed for the whole three hours of the scenic tour, not wanting to move in case we should miss something. Then suddenly, in the late afternoon as our boat makes its way back to the wharf, the perfect ending to a brilliant day comes when we're joined by a pod of bottlenose dolphins riding the bow waves. It's a magical experience and Bob is as thrilled as I am. "I could stay here forever," he says, breathing in deeply and throwing his hands into the air for emphasis. "Look!" he exclaims, "it's absolutely magnificent!" ■

McKenzie Country - Deerace Publishing

TAKE THE SCENIC ROUTE WITH APEX

100% NEW ZEALAND CAR HIRE

WWW.APEXRENTALS.COM

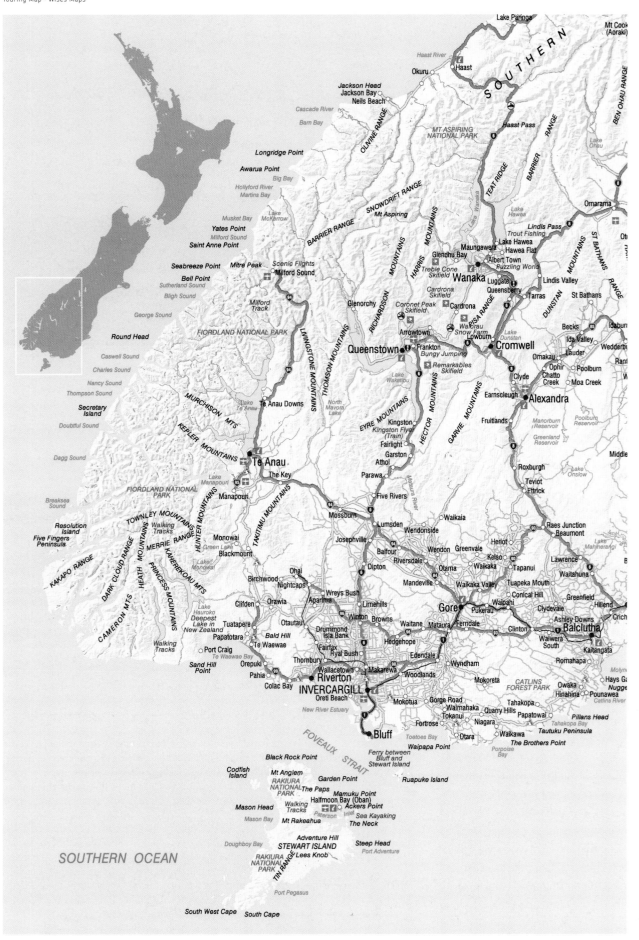

SOUTHERN OCEAN

Wide plains, tussock smothered mountains, rocky tors, clear rivers and opalescent turquoise lakes. This is Central Otago, a region of some 11,000 kilometres squared. It's big sky country where crystal clear light draws mountains closer by day and produces star-studded skies by night.

Upon its plains visitors follow in the footsteps of the hardy 1800s pioneers who flocked here by the thousand to chase their dreams of gold. These early settlers carved a living from the land, transforming its scenery and moving mountains of rock in their quest. Most towns and villages owe their origins to the gold rush, and remnants from this era can be seen in the region's display of cob, mudbrick and stone cottages, and discarded mining equipment scattered throughout the landscape.

Today Central Otago's greatest drawcards are its award winning vineyards, its quaint villages, and historical sites. We spend three days exploring the region and, as well as enjoying local wines, we fish for trout on Lake Dunstan, hike to a deserted mine, stay in a haunted hotel, relax on the shores of St Bathan's Blue Lake, and learn how to pan for gold!

CENTRAL **OTAGO**

DAY ONE
Queenstown to Clyde

Like those who have travelled before us, Bob's eye has a gleam as we leave Queenstown bound for Cromwell. En route we stop to watch brave types defy gravity by plunging 43 metres off the historic Kawerau Suspension Bridge from an architectural masterpiece that blends into the rock walls of the canyon, then continue on to Gibbston Valley Wines. It's nestled in an idyllic setting beneath rocky mountains and here we take a tour of the vineyard and winery, which concludes with a wine tasting in the ambient-lit cool of a dark schist cave cellar.

"Magic," says Bob, as he finishes his taster of Pinot Noir, and we walk to the on-site cheesery, where handcrafted cheeses are made in small batches under the guidance of Gibbston Valley's head chef, Mark Sage. The flavour of the cheese changes subtly with the seasons, and we purchase delicious brie and camembert for the picnic basket before we leave.

On the outskirts of Cromwell we come to a halt outside The Gold Fields Mining Centre where we try our hand at digging and panning for gold. Finders-keepers are the rules and according to our guide Euan Moore most people find a few grains. "Some people have even found whole nuggets," says Euan, laughing as Bob suddenly begins to pan like his life depends on it. The panning takes a bit of practice and I simply don't have enough patience, but Bob picks it up fast and accumulates a few flecks of gold.

After several unsuccessful attempts I leave Bob to it and instead spend time enjoying the displays of old mining equipment including gravity fed sluice guns and stamping batteries, before wandering through the replica miner's cottages and Chinese village.

When I return Bob has a wild gleam in his eye and it's clear that a few grains aren't going to be enough to satisfy his gold fever. "Won't be long," he calls out cheerfully as he begins another pan.

An hour later my patience is well beyond thin. Reluctantly Bob leaves his pan behind and grumbles "I'll be back," to Euan as he passes by.

He stares sullenly at his glass gold vial all the way to Bannockburn, where only the magical outlook from Mt Difficulty Wines breaks him from his reverie. We dine upon the terrace which offers sweeping views of the vineyard and Bannockburn; I enjoy a Bruschetta Platter which teams beautifully with a glass of Long Gully Reisling, while Bob makes short work of a rare beef sandwich with an accompanying glass of pinot noir.

"We'll stop for more gold panning on our way back to Queenstown," I promise Bob as his mood slowly improves over lunch.

Then we drive to Cromwell where stone-fruit and apple orchards abound, and juicy nectarines, apricots and peaches are ripe for the picking. Saritas provides us with a bag of each before we continue on to Old Cromwell Town, relocated to the 'new' lake shore by a proactive group of locals who saved the town's historic buildings when it was demolished to make way for the hydro-lake. Entry is free and the 'old town' is now home to local craftspeople and a café; we take a look around then relax on the beautiful turquoise shores of Lake Dunstan soaking up the sun before meeting up with local trout fishing guide Dick Marquand.

An ex Fish and Game officer, Dick operates as a catch and release guide on local rivers but he considers the lake fair game. "You can get three fish an hour," he says as we climb aboard, and true to his word we do! They're short and fat but Dick says they make good eating because they feed upon a tasty soft footed snail.

We throw them back as we already have dinner plans and drive south east along the Clutha River to Clyde where we come face to face with NZ's third largest hydro generating station – the Clyde Dam. "Wow," says Bob as we stand at the lookout. This mammoth structure is built from 1.2 million cubic metres of concrete.

Below is the sleepy village of Clyde where, once we've checked into Oliver's Lodge and Restaurant, we set off to explore its wealth of historic buildings including the old courthouse, post office and offices of Dunstan News, then finish up with a stroll along the river.

Back at Oliver's, housed inside the town's old 1863 Calico general store, we are served a delicious seared venison dish followed by rich ricotta cake and poached plums for dessert, seated beside a huge schist fireplace surrounded by cobbled floors and heavy beams. Later we retire to the rustic charm of our luxuriously renovated stable room and fall asleep dreaming of days of old.

DAY TWO
Clyde to St Bathans

In the morning after a hearty breakfast served in the dining room of Oliver's charming homestead, we drive through Alexandra and on to historic Ophir. We reach this small settlement via a majestic suspension bridge built in 1880 prior to the Ophir gold rush of 1863. Back then the town boasted several stores as well as a school, police station, courthouse, post office, cottage hospital and doctor. We stop to admire these buildings, before driving on back roads through the Raggedy Range to Poolburn and onto Oturehua where we call into Hayes Engineering Works, established in 1895 by Ernest Hayes, an English engineer. Hayes invented several farm tools including the parallel wire strainer which is still used on modern farms today. We tour the plant which comprises several buildings and a windmill used to power his works, then head to Oturehua's old store as Bob has a hankering for some gum.

"Wow, some store," remarks Bob, as he heaves open a heavy green wooden door to a large warehouse which still has its original kauri counters, shelves and roll-a-door containers.

Gum purchased, we drive along Reefs Rd and walk to the Golden Progress Mine, where poised some 46 metres above the mine shaft is Otago's only remaining example of a poppet

Central Otago Area:
Attractions and Activities

Goldfields Mining Centre: www.cromwell.org.nz/goldfields.index/html
Shotover Jet: www.shotoverjet.co.nz
Kawarau Bridge Bungy Jump: www.ajhackett.com
Kayak and Mountain Biking: www.trailjourneys.co.nz
Safari Excursions: www.wildflowerwalks.co.nz
Maniototo Ice Rink: www.maniototo.co.nz
Dick Marquand Trout Fishing: www.troutfishingservices.co.nz
Old Cromwell Town: www.cromwell.org.nz
Hayes Engineering Works: www.nzmuseums.co.nz
Touch Yarns: www.touchyarns.com

Central Otago Area:
Cafés and Eateries

Bannockburn Heights Café: Cairnmuir Rd, Bannockburn
Gibbston Valley Vineyard and Café: Gibbston Valley, Queenstown
La Strada Café: Centennial Ave, Alexandra
Olivers: Sunderland St, Clyde
Vulcan Hotel: Main Rd, St Bathans
Shaky Bridge Café: William Hill Wines, Alexandra
Black Ridge Vineyard: Conroys Rd, Alexandra

> Bob has a wild gleam to his eye and it's clear that a few grains aren't going to be enough to satisfy his gold fever

head, a contraption used to hoist gold bearing ore to the surface.

Hunger forces us to leave the mine and continue on to Ranfurly, passing Wedderburn's famous goods shed en route, retrieved from the Mt Ida Coal Mine by locals who were inspired by Grahame Sydney's painting "July on the Maniototo" depicting the shed beside the Central Otago Rail Trail.

We admire Ranfurly's wealth of art deco buildings, built in the 1930s after fire destroyed much of this historic goldmining town, while eating chicken and egg sandwiches at traditional kiwi tearooms on the main street.

The town became the railhead for the district in December 1898, providing a link between Dunedin and Central Otago's gold field towns. Later the railway was extended to Alexandra, Clyde and Cromwell; today the railroad has been transformed into a 150 km long recreational Rail Trail suitable for hiking, horse riding and mountain biking.

The latter is a popular sport in the nearby village of Naseby, where

Bob and I are greeted by a sign: "Welcome to Naseby - 2000 feet above worry level".

"Isn't that the whole of NZ?" questions Bob as we explore the historic cob and mudbrick buildings of this quaint goldmining town then pass the Naseby Forest where mountain biking enthusiasts congregate ready to tackle its trails.

In the winter an ice skating rink provides entertainment and the friendly lady manning the information centre tells us that curling, an old Scottish game akin to bowls on ice, is held here from June through to August.

It's mid afternoon so we backtrack on SH85 to Hills Creek then shortly after turn off for St Bathans, an old goldmining town nestled beside the Blue Lake Recreational Reserve. This tiny town has a permanent population of only five residents even though there's many attractions including a stunning blue lake (dug by miners!), the famous Vulcan Hotel and several other notable buildings including the Bank of New South Wales Gold Office and Despatches, the old Post Office that now sells Victorian-style gifts. "It's a real privilege to live here," says Sharon Hinds when we call in.

We relax beside the beautiful sapphire waters of Blue Lake with its sculpted whitestone cliffs, then with some trepidation check into the Vulcan Hotel. It was built in 1882 from sun dried bricks, and rumour has it there is a resident ghost. Our hosts offer us the renovated Constable Cottage but Bob, eager to see if the ghost story is true, insists we stay in the hotel. As punishment I make him take the haunted room, while I ensconce myself in a ghost-free room next door! "Some say it's an Australian goldminer, but most say it's a girl with long brown hair," says Jude Kavangh, the publican's wife. "I haven't seen her but she's not scary, just a tad naughty – she likes to hide things from time to time."

After dinner and several glasses of 'Dog's Nose', an old shearer's drink, at the bar, Bob's full of Dutch courage while I'm simply ready for bed. "Good luck!" I whisper at the door before I climb into my comfortable bed and fall immediately asleep.

Felton Rd Vineyard - Destination Queenstown

DAY THREE
St Bathans to Queenstown

"Bugger!" exclaims Bob in the morning, mimicking a shearer from the bar. "I fell asleep straight away."

After a light continental breakfast and an hour spent basking in the sun at the lake, we follow SH85 through numerous tiny settlements to Alexandra where we enjoy an early lunch at the Shaky Bridge Café beside William Hill Vineyard. Above, high on the rocky schist hillside overlooking the town, the Alexandra Clock beckons and so after lunch we follow a steep track through rocky schist, where the sweet aroma of wild thyme fills the air, to the lookout for views of the clock and town.

Then we drive across the magnificent Alexandra Bridge over the Clutha River, with its banks smothered in willows and poplar trees. A three-hour hike follows the river to Clyde but we take the back road, stopping at Black Ridge Vineyard where we meet Sue Edwards and her partner Verdun Burgess. This intrepid pair pioneered wine in the region when they planted their vines in 1981. "It wasn't fashionable then," said Sue, pouring us a tasting of their well known pinot noir and gewürztraminer. The pinot noir was so successful others invested and today there are many vineyards in this, the world's southernmost winemaking region. We purchase a couple of bottles to join our burgeoning collection in the boot, then call into nearby Touch Yarns to admire Marnie Kelly's handiwork: designer garments made from her own dyed wools that reflect the vivid shades of Central Otago's great outdoors. I buy a gorgeous mohair hat, the exact shade of autumnal poplars, before we drive to the old gold mining tailings beside the river.

"It's hard to believe that they moved all this rock," says Bob as we walk over literally mountains of gravel and rock to reach the river, passing mountain bikers crisscrossing on well formed tracks.

We return to Cromwell where I stop and make a purchase while Bob awaits my return in the car. On the outskirts of town we come to a halt outside The Gold Fields Mining Centre. Bob turns to beam at me. "Fill your boots!" I say waving my newly purchased book, "There's three hours until they close." ■

At latitude 45 degrees south, Central Otago is the southernmost commercial wine region in the world. Its vineyards huddle beneath the jagged schist rock mountains of the Southern Alps, well protected from coastal winds. At around 300 metres above sea level – with many vineyards clinging to the sides of steep river gorges – it's also New Zealand's highest wine-growing area.

Hot, dry summers and crisp snowy winters provide a climate similar to other great wine regions around the world including Burgundy, Alsace and the Willamette Valley in Oregon. Relatively low annual rainfall reduces the need for spraying and there is a low incidence of fungal disease.

The hot, dry summer days teamed with cool temperatures at night allow the grapes to ripen slowly and give the wines an intense, pure flavour, while the soil structure, which differs considerably from other grape-growing regions in NZ, is heavy with mineral deposits of mica and schist in a silt loam and provides excellent drainage. All in all, despite the occasional frost, perfect conditions are provided for the creation of high quality Pinot Noir, Chardonnay, Pinot Gris and Riesling.

Central Otago's first wines were produced in the 19th century when miners were lured here by the gleam of gold. The first Mayor of Clyde, Jean Desire Feraud, won awards for his wines in Australia in the 1880s, and the gold miners themselves planted many grapevines. However, despite the region being acknowledged as having suitable wine growing potential, the early wine industry did not survive. It wasn't until the late 1970s and early 1980s that there was a revival in grapes with the planting of the Rippon Vineyard in Wanaka, Gibbston Valley Wines in Queenstown and Black Ridge in Alexandra.

COOL CLIMATE WINE

For the visitor today, Central Otago's golden tussock hills, dramatic river gorges, wide plains, turquoise lakes, rocky schist tors, and jagged mountain scenery make it a most memorable wine trail destination.

There are four sub-regions within Central Otago to visit: Gibbston Valley, Cromwell/Bannockburn, Wanaka and Alexandra. Wine connoisseurs can look forward to several days of touring the countryside.

The Gibbston Valley offers wines as dramatic as the landscape itself, and there's an opportunity to sample wine in the candlelit ambience of a deep schist cave-turned-wine-cellar at Gibbston Valley Wines. This vineyard also offers gorgeous vineyard dining, and a menu that reflects the lifestyle of the region through dishes such as vine-smoked venison, saddle of rabbit and poached rump of lamb. Tours are held on the hour and visitors are shown through the vineyard and winery, finishing with a wine tasting in NZ's largest underground wine cave. Although the vineyard's focus is on Pinot Noir (its 2000 Reserve Pinot Noir won the 2001 International Wine Challenge in London), newer projects such as the on-site cheesery have also proved popular and complement wine-tasting trays.

The Cromwell/Bannockburn wine trail passes through stunning mountain scenery with vineyards planted on the banks of the dramatic Kawarau River Gorge and sparkling turquoise waters of Lake Dunstan. Vineyards such as Mt Difficulty (one of the region's high profile labels) and Carrick Vineyard, which offers views splendid views of the rugged mountains of the Carrick Range, provide the opportunity to dine, while others such as Olssens encourage visitors to picnic amongst their vines.

The Wanaka wine trail provides a boutique winery experience at vineyards including Rippon Vineyard on the edge of picturesque Lake Wanaka, as well known for its stunning location and vineyard scenery as it is for its Pinot Noir, the region's most commonly grown varietal. This intrepid vineyard produced the region's first sparkling wine and first botryised Riesling and also produces Sauvignon Blanc, Gewürztraminer, Osteiner, Gamay Rose, Hotere White and a Merlot Syrah blend.

The Clyde/Alexander wine trail features some ten wineries, plus a fascinating look into the region's gold mining heritage. The dry, rocky soil that used to be mined for precious metal now yields a liquid gold harvest at vineyards such as Black Ridge, established by Sue Edwards and Verdun Burgess in 1981 and the most southern vineyard and winery in the world. Black Ridge offers a blended wine, Earnscleugh Rise, which makes popular summer time drinking, but the extreme temperatures experienced in Alexandra provide an ideal climate for growing and ripening classic wine varietals including Gewürztraminer, Riesling, Pinot Noir, Chardonnay and Cabernet Sauvignon. ■

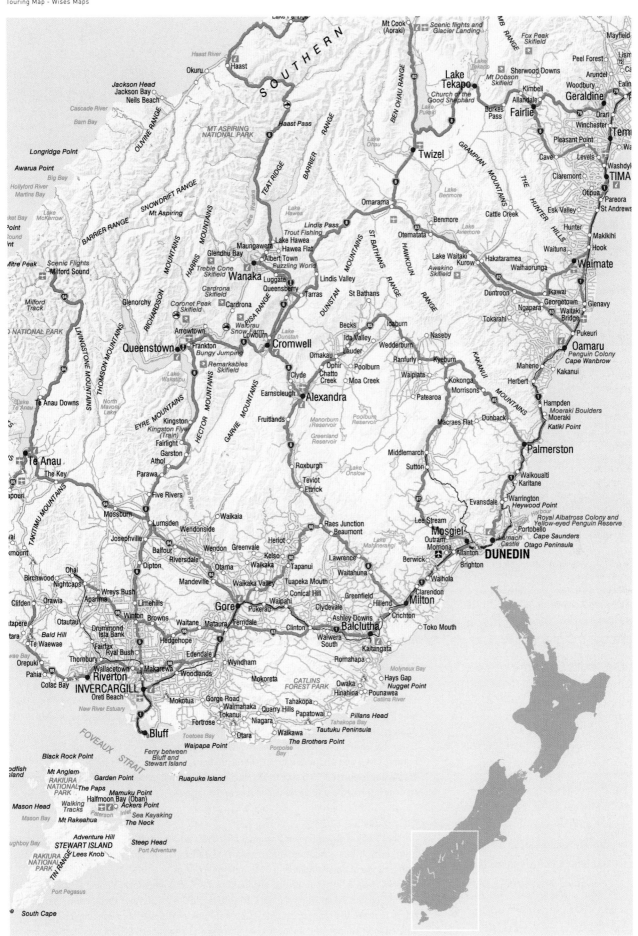

In the winter, the Southern Lakes region of the South Island is transformed into a magical wonderland with perfect powder snow covering the slopes of the surrounding mountain ranges. Ski fields open and skiers and snowboarders from far and wide dust off their snowboards, wax their skis, and come out to play. Planning a ski or snowboard holiday in this region is stress free as New Zealand provides accommodation and transport to suit every budget and there are four ski fields located close to Queenstown and Wanaka: Coronet Peak, Cardrona, Treble Cone, and the Remarkables. Each provides the skier and boarder with a range of terrain, facilities and scenery. Heli-skiing, popular in these parts, provides the opportunity to escape the crowds and traverse unmarked snow. It's a sport more suited to intermediate and advanced skiers and there's thousands of square kilometres of private terrain to choose from.

SKIING AND SNOWBOARDING

Nestled on the shores of Lake Wakatipu and completely surrounded by breathtaking snow-capped mountains, Queenstown celebrates the snowy season with its annual Winter Festival. It's an event that is well known as the Southern Hemisphere's ultimate winter party and it provides more than 70 events in town and on the slopes which range from wild and wacky to glamourous and cultural. To complement your winter ski holiday there's a wide range of adventure activities also on offer and with over 100 bars, cafés and restaurants as well as a multitude of other relaxing après ski options, Queenstown is the place to be during the winter.

The Queenstown ski season kicks off in June with the opening of Coronet Peak Ski Resort, which offers a variety of terrain to suit all levels of ability and boasts the Southern Hemisphere's largest snowmaking capacity, ensuring optimum conditions throughout the season.

Across town the gentle slopes of The Remarkables ski area, which hosts the annual Remarkables Spring Festival, provides stunning views of Queenstown. Family-oriented, there's plenty of challenge for even the most advanced skier and rider, with powder bowls and off-piste mountain riding complemented by the Xbox Terrain Park and Superpipe.

Less than an hour's drive away is Wanaka, a relaxed alpine town with two major ski areas plus The Snowfarm, NZ's only Nordic area, and the Snowpark, a dedicated freestyle area. Additionally there are several heli-ski runs.

Cardrona, the 'snowboarders' capital' provides four boarding parks and has 100 per cent natural snow and undulating trails that span across 320 hectares of land.

Treble Cone, dubbed TC by the locals, is a steep mountain providing a range of exciting terrain for intermediate to advanced skiers and boarders.

CORONET PEAK

Coronet Peak is Queenstown's original ski resort and is situated a mere 25 minutes drive from town. It has a reputation for some of the most varied ski landscapes in Australasia with a range of open slopes and wide rolling terrain.

Coronet Peak hosts high profile events such as The Queenstown Winter Festival and the 50K of Coronet Peak. Night skiing, currently exclusive to Coronet Peak, allows skiers and riders to make the most of each day. Coronet Peak's extensive snowmaking facilities guarantee a long season and its award winning ski and snowboard school provides lessons for learners and assistance for those wanting to hone rusty skills.

THE REMARKABLES

On the other side of the valley lies The Remarkables, a friendly and relaxed ski field well suited to families. Children have the use of Skiwiland, and those ten years and under get a free day lift pass. Surrounded by towering peaks, The Remarkables offers three sunny sheltered bowls and is a great place to learn to ski as there is easy access to the learner runs. There's also a variety of challenging terrain on offer as well as long off-piste runs.

CARDRONA

Cardrona, rated after extensive research by the Ski Areas Association of NZ (SANZ) as New Zealand's leading ski area, offers varied terrain and reliable natural snow which attracts all levels of skiers and boarders from beginners to advanced.

It is home to New Zealand's longest terrain park, which provides some 25 features set over a 1.3 kilometre course, and it has the Southern Hemisphere's largest pipe park with four half and super pipes. The half pipes have reinforced Cardrona's position as an internationally recognised freestyle destination.

High profile events held at Cardrona include the Burton New Zealand Open, when the world's top professional snowboarders put on a spectacular display of competitive riding in the superpipe and terrain park; the New Zealand National Ski Championships; and the National Snowboard Championships.

Cardrona is also popular with families as it provides a comprehensive range of children's programmes and facilities catering for children aged from three months to 12 years of age.

TREBLE CONE

Treble Cone, the Southern Hemisphere's training ground of choice for European and US World Cup national teams, is the South Island's largest ski area. Its slopes are uncrowded and it provides reliable snow conditions with a variety of runs, including Australasia's longest groomed trail at seven kilometres in length. The ski field is set on 550 hectares of terrain and offers a premium winter snow experience with world-famous views across Lake Wanaka and Mt Aspiring.

The installation of a new quad chairlift, which transports visitors to 'Tim's Table' at 1950 metres in the popular saddle basin area, has expanded intermediate terrain by a further 45 hectares.

In the latest survey by SANZ, Treble Cone was rated tops for its alpine cuisine, snow school and mountain hire equipment.

HELI-SKIING

If the thought of escaping the crowds and carving unmarked snow sounds appealing, then heliskiing, the ultimate alpine adventure, is for you! From glaciers to gentle runs there's a diverse range of terrain on offer for the keen heli-skiier or rider in the Southern Lakes region. Using the helicopter as a chairlift, groups consisting of four to five plus a guide are dropped on exclusive mountain ranges at altitudes of between 1400 and 2200 metres where they traverse unadulterated snow before they're picked up by helicopter and transported to another unique location.

Let Ski New Zealand Online organise your next New Zealand ski or snowboard holiday. Holidays packages start from as low as NZD99 per person per day.

Ski New Zealand is New Zealand's premier booking site for all Ski-Queenstown, Ski-Wanaka, and Ski- Canterbury package holidays.

When you book your ski holiday with Ski New Zealand there are no hidden costs. All prices are quoted in New Zealand dollars and include GST (NZ Sales Tax).

All Ski New Zealand packages include:

- Your choice of ski area (or areas) including Queenstown, Wanaka and Canterbury
- Your choice of accommodation style from backpacker hostels to 5-star luxury apartments
- Your choice of car hire or mountain coach transfers.
- Your choice of ski/snowboard passes and equipment/clothing hire.

All packages also offer the option of commencing your holiday at Christchurch, Queenstown, or Dunedin.

Organising your Ski-New Zealand Holiday is simple, cost effective and fast. Simply visit their website at www.ski-newzealand.co.nz and request an online quote, or call their Central Reservations freephone number direct.

From within New Zealand dial 0800 500 660

From Australia dial 1800 121 029

From all other countries dial +64 3 379 1451

From the ice-blue waters of Lake Wanaka to the grandeur of the Haast Pass, SH6 cuts a winding route through dense forest in Mt Aspiring National Park, before continuing on up the spectacular West Coast of the South Island. This epic journey provides the traveller with fresh inspiration at every turn. Here, where towering rainforests, rugged mountains, icy glaciers, and rivers meet a moody, ever-changing shore, the friendly West Coaster, a hardy, creative type of New Zealander, makes his home.

We take four days to explore the route from Queenstown to Greymouth. We kick start our journey with a horse trek in the Cardrona Valley, then Bob takes an impromptu Spitfire flight and I tease my brain at Puzzling World in Wanaka. Together we join a thrilling jet boat ride on the Waiatoto River, admire Mt Cook's sunset reflection in Lake Matheson, do a challenging hike on Franz Josef glacier, spy on nesting herons, dine on fresh whitebait and a unique possum stew, and in the manner of true West Coasters, wash it all down with a jug of Monteiths!

QUEENSTOWN TO GREYMOUTH

DAY ONE
Queenstown to Wanaka

It's 10.30 am in the Cardrona Valley and ahead of me Bob teeters precariously atop an extremely well-behaved Appaloosa which picks its way sedately along a trail to the top of a ridge. The views of the dry, rounded, tussock-filled landscape below are incredible.
"This isn't so bad," he says, in reference to the ride. "I'm glad I gave it a go!"
Bob left his comfort zone to join me on this ride with Backcountry Saddle Expeditions but somehow I think it was the well-timed comments of our guide, Debbie Thompson, about western saddles and cowboys that really piqued his interest. Debbie, an intriguing southern belle who appears in Kevyn Male's book, Grassroots Kiwi, amuses us on the descent with her lively banter. Apparently she and her husband (none other than the Speights billboard man!) bought the business when he grew tired of dragging home deer he'd shot in the bush. A horse was required and when they went to find a suitable steed, they ended up with several Appaloosas. "I've been riding ever since," says Debbie as we depart, well satisfied with our ride.
After enjoying lunch overlooking Lake Wanaka, we check into our accommodation, then Bob and I go our separate ways. He drives to the Wanaka Transport and Toy Museum where there's an interesting collection of rare and unusual aircraft, trucks, motorcycles, fire engines, tractors and military vehicles. It's also the site of the Southern Hemisphere's best-regarded vintage air-show, Warbirds over Wanaka, held bi-annually over Easter. Meanwhile I venture to Puzzling World to put my grey matter to the test with its array of crazy architecture and brain teasers. Then, once I've had my fill, I walk back into town and relax at our accommodation by the lake.
Bob returns in the late afternoon and over dinner at the Tuatara Pizza Company he's still buzzing. In true Bob-fashion he struck a rapport with an enthusiast who took him for a ride in his Spitfire. "It was amazing, you should have seen it go!"

DAY TWO
Wanaka to Franz Josef

We leave Wanaka early and drive north on SH6, past the still, reflective waters of Lake Hawea and on through thick rainforest in the magnificent Haast Pass. True to form it's raining – cats and dogs!

"Wow," says Bob, opening the window then shutting it abruptly as he's hit by a deluge, "this really is RAINforest."

We continue on to Haast keeping the windows firmly closed and just as we ready ourselves to dive into the information centre the rain stops as abruptly as it started and out comes the sun. It's perfect timing: just in time for a spin in a jet boat on the Waiatoto River. Before we board, our skilled jetboat guide Roger Crow passes out lifejackets and swandries – a warm woollen jacket favoured by NZ farming folk – and we climb aboard. It's a thrilling ride packed with spins and whitewater excitement, and en route Roger names the mountains of the Haast and the Selbourne Ranges and provides a commentary on the local area. We pass several interesting sites including the alpine fault line where botanists have discovered trees growing slower than elsewhere, and a place where Haast kiwi, the only alpine species, are protected then released into the wild by Dept. of Conservation.

Afterwards we eat filled rolls at Fantail Café then cross the Haast River Bridge, the longest single-lane bridge in NZ. Before the bridge was built travellers would set off explosives to attract the attention of a rower, who would fetch them across the river. Local legend tells of the rower being held hostage by those isolated in the north who were keen to catch up on world news!

And there's no doubt that we're in a remote corner of the world. Few other cars pass and those who do, wave. Bob gets into the spirit of things and pre-empts their greetings on the drive to Lake Moeraki, where we stop to stretch our legs then continue on through towering kahikatea forest to Fox Glacier township, nestled in the shadow of the glacier's icy tongue. We call into the DOC centre where there are some extremely informative display boards describing the forming of the glaciers, and then, after checking into our accommodation, we hike the Chalet Lookout Walk crossing several streams to a viewpoint that gives magical views of the lower icefall. On our return we debate whether to do a guided glacier hike on Fox or Franz Josef Glacier – in the end Franz Josef wins out. Back in the village, we pick up takeaways then drive to Lake Matheson for a picnic dinner. Here we admire perfect sunset views of the summit of Mt Cook and Fox Glacier mirrored in the waters of the lake before carefully making our way back through still forest in the dark, guided by our flashlights.

DAY THREE
Franz Josef to Hokitika

In the morning we take SH6 north and half an hour later arrive in Franz Josef. It's somewhat larger and definitely busier than its nearby cousin and as rain threatens, we dash into Franz Josef Glacier Guides to check that the glacier hike is still on. It is, and so we emerge wearing standard glacier hiking gear: a Gore-Tex jacket, socks, boots and gloves. A short bus ride leads us to the start of the track. Back in 1930 this was the base of the glacier; today it's a three-kilometre hike!

En route our informative and friendly guide, Rob Knox, tells us that Franz Josef is the world's steepest and fastest-flowing commercially guided glacier. "The glacier's head receives enormous amounts of snow which 'drive' the glacier at speeds of up to ten metres per day," he says.

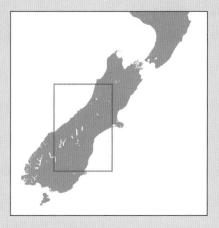

Queenstown to Greymouth:
Attractions and Activities

Backcountry Saddle: www.ridenz.com
Waitoto River Safaris: www.riversafaris.co.nz
Alpine Guides: www.foxguides.co.nz
Franz Josef Glacier Guides: www.explorefranzjosef.com
Fox and Franz Heliservices: www.scenic-flights.co.nz
Ferg's Kayaks: www.glacierkayaks.com
White Heron Sanctuary Tours: www.whiteherontours.co.nz
Scenic Waterways: www.paddleboatcruises.com
Shantytown: www.shantytown.co.nz
Monteiths Brewing Co: www.monteiths.co.nz

Queenstown to Greymouth:
Cafés and Eateries

Tuatara Pizza Co: Ardmore St, Wanaka
Ritual Espresso Bar: Helwick St, Wanaka
Café Lake Matheson: Lake Matheson Rd, Fox Glacier
Fantail Café: Marks Road, Haast
Beeches Restaurant: SH6, Franz Josef
Café de Paris: Tancred St, Hokitika
DP:One Café: Mawhera Quay, Greymouth

> " We relax amid lavender
> and topiary beach-stone
> gardens, in a pair of kermit-
> green gas-fired bath tubs
> overlooking the ocean "

The weight of the snow compresses into glacier ice, which melts and forms tunnels which carry the ice-melt away.

At the base of the glacier – it looks really slippery – we strap 'Ice Talonz' over our boots for grip. Bob dances on the spot then topples as his feet touch and the Talonz catch.

Slowly and with an ungainly gait, we begin to make our way up the face of the glacier. At first it's pretty scary, but we gain confidence and before long we're scruffing our Talonz firmly into the ice and walking "positively" as instructed by Rob.

And it's just as well for soon the descent begins through stunning, icy-blue tunnels and past deep crevasses which emit incredibly intense shades of blue – even on a dull day like today. It's such fun that our four-and-a-half hour tour seems to pass by in a flash and before we know it we're back in town.

After hungrily wolfing down lunch at Beeches we drive past Lake Mapourika (famous for its trout and salmon) and Lake Wahapo en route to Whataroa, which boasts NZ's only nesting colony of white heron.

Here we join a small group aboard a jet boat and after following the Waitangitaona and Waitangiroto Rivers, we land at a small jetty surrounded by towering kahikatea forest. Our White Heron Sanctuary Tour guide, Deon, leads us along a boardwalk to a hide from which we have perfect views of these magnificent birds sitting on their nests across the river. Amongst other interesting facts, Deon tells us that the herons arrive in early September to breed and the nearby Okarito Lagoon provides a plentiful supply of food.

Spotting a rare royal spoonbill Bob thinks it's a heron with a deformed beak. "Oh no," laughs Deon, "we've also got 30 royal spoonbill nests."

At 3 pm we hit the road again, driving north to the small township of Harihari, past Lake Ianthe and on to Ross, home to the famous Ross Goldfields. NZ's largest gold nugget was unearthed here in 1909. It weighed 3.6 kilograms and was presented to King George V as a coronation present. We stretch our legs on the tailings by the river and then continue on to Hokitika where we treat ourselves to a stay at Villa Polenza, high on an escarpment overlooking the town and an endless stretch of ocean.

Our true-blue West Coast hosts, Russell and Trina Diedrich, serve us a perfect dinner of skewered whitebait fritters (the best I've ever tasted), followed by French racks of lamb marinated in fresh rosemary, crushed garlic and olive oil, washed down with a bottle of Centago Pinot Noir 2002, grown on Trina's family's vineyard in Alexandra. After dinner we relax amid lavender and topiary beach-stone gardens, in a pair of Kermit-green gas-fired bath tubs overlooking the ocean. "Bliss," says Bob, as we watch the heavens for our chance to wish upon a falling star.

DAY FOUR
Hokitika to Greymouth

Today it's a short drive from Hokitika to Greymouth and so after a light breakfast in-house we spend the morning exploring the jade galleries and studios of Hokitika's talented artisans. The town's range of raw materials – jade, gold, timber, clay, shell, bone and fibres – combined with its inspiring surrounds has produced a vibrant arts community

Ice Tunnel - Donna Blaber

and we join others who zigzag between the studios of glassblowers, jewellers, woodturners and potters.

We enjoy coffee on a sunny pavement outside Café de Paris, then after viewing the displays at The West Coast Historical Museum, housed inside the historic Carnegie Complex, we pop into Jacquie Grant's Eco World to see – amongst other creatures – her rare collection of NZ long-finned eels, most of which are over 100 years old.

Before leaving town we enjoy a tasty possum stew at Trappers, Hokitika's original wild food restaurant, where Bob learns all about the town's annual Wild Foods Festival held in March. It's well known for its untamed gastronomic creativity and the festival provides all manner of culinary delights – everything from eel stew to worm sushi is up for grabs!

Then we drive towards Greymouth, crossing rivers that are lined with the tell-tale huts of whitebaiters, and turn off for Shantytown, shortly after Kumara Junction. "Wow," exclaims Bob, as we're transported back to the 1860s gold rush in this replica West Coast settlement. There are more than 30 historic buildings to see including a sawmill, stables, bank, hotel, barber's shop, miners' hall, printing works and blacksmith.

We take a ride on one of Shantytown's steam trains, the 25-ton Kaitangata, built in 1897. Its tracks follow the route of an old sawmill tramline, and like many of the first bush tramways in NZ, it was originally wooden railed and worked by horses. Steel rails and steam locomotives became common from 1900, when bushmen began to work steeper country further from the mills.

On the return journey Bob's eyes light up when he spots an opportunity to pan for gold even though he had more than his fair share in Central Otago. Scott Arnold provides expert instruction but Bob's already well versed; however when he discovers Scott's a champion gold panner and can shake a Shantytown pan down in nine seconds flat (which he proves) Bob goes hard out to try and beat his time – to no avail!

It's another ten kilometres into Greymouth and here we end the day at Monteith's Brewery, where we watch every step of the brewing process from malting through to bottling. The highlight comes at the end when we get to sit down and taste Monteith's range of thirst-quenching and naturally fermented beers.

"It's a great way to end any day on the West Coast," says our tour guide to Bob, who responds by taking a deep slug on his glass of Monteith's Black. He then wipes its froth from his bristling upper lip with a quick brush of his sleeve like a wild West Coast goldminer of old, and growls: "Sure is." ∎

COFFEE
SUPREME

Relax at Wellington's Olive Café or any one of New Zealand's top cafes serving Coffee Supreme and you can rest assured that you'll be served a consistently fresh, rich and full-bodied signature blend of medium dark espresso roasted coffee, every time. Cafés serving Coffee Supreme are located through New Zealand and range from winery cafés employing world-class chefs to trendy suburban brasseries and your inner-city "hole-in-the-wall" espresso bar.

As well as serving New Zealand's favourite coffee bean, these cafés all share a passion for great NZ cuisine.

Often described as 'Pacific Rim', and drawing inspiration from Asia, Polynesia and Europe, modern New Zealand cuisine can be experienced in a mouthwatering range of flavours and foods at cafés and restaurants throughout the country. With the finest range of fresh local foods and seasonal produce readily available, New Zealand's chefs are spoilt for choice. Local dishes are inspired by NZ lamb and venison and kai moana (seafood) including crayfish, mussels, Bluff oysters and salmon. Alongside perfect strawberries and juicy sun filled citrus, you may encounter feijoa, tamarillo and, of course, kiwifruit. Less common indigenous foods such as kumara (sweet potato), puha (watercress) and pipis and tua tua (species of NZ shellfish) and flavourings such as horopito (native pepper) have progressively made their way onto café menus.

New Zealanders have embraced the café lifestyle, which perfectly complements the relaxed and friendly kiwi psyche. Al fresco meals such as picnics at scenic locations and barbecues form a distinctive part of the kiwi culture and there's no better way to spend a lazy summer afternoon than relaxing outdoors at your favourite Coffee Supreme café, enjoying a tasty array of tantalising local cuisine.

For further information on Coffee Supreme or to search for cafés and locations nationwide serving this richly complex and full bodied espresso, please visit www.coffeesupreme.co.nz.

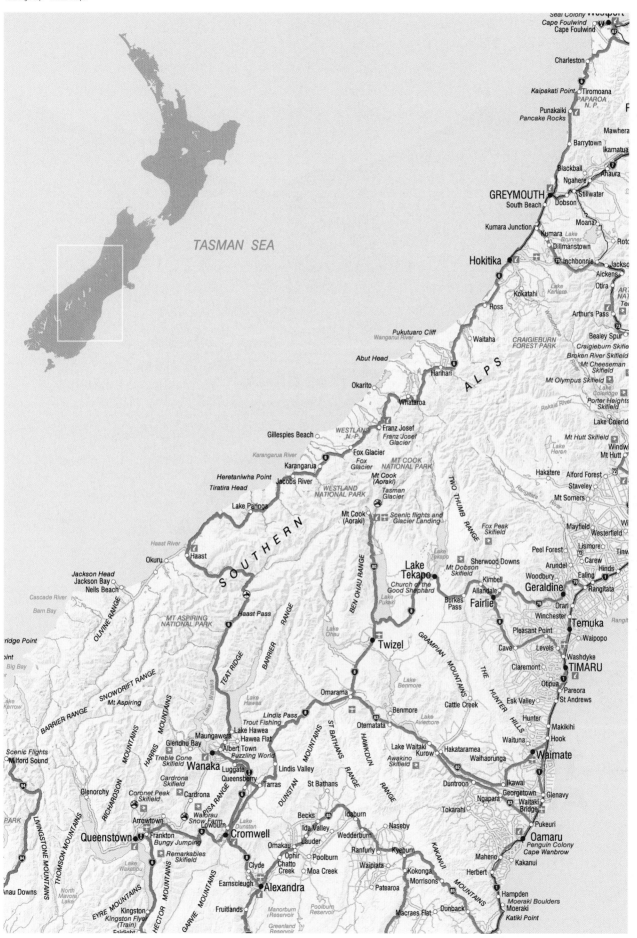

TASMAN SEA

Seal Colony·Westport
Cape Foulwind
Cape Foulwind

Charleston

Kaipakati Point·Tiromoana
PAPAROA
N. P.
Punakaiki
Pancake Rocks

Mawhera

Barrytown
Ikamatua

Blackball
Ngahere Ahaura
GREYMOUTH·Stillwater
South Beach Dobson
Moana
Kumara Junction
Kumara Lake
Brunner Roto
Dillmanstown
Hokitika Inchbonnie Jackso
Aickens
Kokatahi Lake
Kaniere Otira ART
NAT
Ross Ter
Arthur's Pass
Waitaha Bealey Spur
Pukutuaro Cliff CRAIGIEBURN
Wanganui River FOREST PARK
Craigieburn Skifiel
Abut Head Harihari Broken River Skifield
Mt Cheeseman
A L P S Skifield
Okarito Mt Olympus Skifield
Whataroa Lake
Coleridge
Porter Heights
Franz Josef Skifield
Gillespies Beach Franz Josef Lake Colerid
Glacier Rakaid River
WESTLAND
N.P. Mt Hutt Skifield
Fox Glacier
Karangarua River Fox Mt Hutt Windwh
Karangarua Glacier MT COOK
NATIONAL PARK Lake
Heron
Heretaniwha Point Mt Cook Hakatere Alford Forest
Tiratira Head Jacobs River (Aoraki) Staveley
WESTLAND Tasman Mt Somers
NATIONAL PARK Glacier Rangitata
Lake Paringa Mayfield Westerfield
Mt Cook Scenic flights and River
(Aoraki) Glacier Landing Lismore
Peel Forest Carew
Haast River Mt Dobson Arundel Ealing
Okuru Haast Skifield Woodbury Hinds
Fox Peak Lake
Skifield Tekapo
S O U T H E R N Lake Tekapo Sherwood Downs Geraldine Rangitata
Church of the Kimbell
Good Shepherd Allandale Orari Temuka
Jackson Head Burkes Fairlie Winchester Rangit
Jackson Bay Pass
Neils Beach Lake Pleasant Point
Cascade River Pukaki Cave Waipopo
Barn Bay MT ASPIRING Haast Pass Levels
NATIONAL PARK Claremont TIMARU
Lake Twizel Washdyke
Ohau Otipua
ridge Point Pareora
Point GRAMPIAN Esk Valley St Andrews
Big Bay Lake MOUNTAINS
Benmore Hunter
Mt Aspiring THE
Omarama Makikihi
HUNTER
SNOWDRIFT RANGE Lake Waituna Hook
Benmore
Lindis Pass Cattle Creek HILLS
BARRIER RANGE Trout Fishing Benmore Waimate
Scenic Flights Otematata
Milford Sound Lake Hawea Lake Waitaki Waihaorunga
Maungawera Hawea Flat Awakino
Albert Town Skifield Duntroon Ikawai
Glendhu Bay Puzzling World Georgetown Glenavy
Treble Cone Lindis Valley Ngapara Waitaki
Skifield Wanaka Bridge
Cardrona Luggate Tokarahi Pukeuri
Glenorchy Skifield Queensberry Becks Idaburn
Coronet Peak Cardrona Tarras Ida Valley Oamaru
Skifield Lindis Valley Naseby Penguin Colony
Arrowtown Waiorau St Bathans Maheno Cape Wanbrow
Snow Farm Lauder Wedderburn
Cowburn Lake Kakanui
Queenstown Frankton Cromwell Dunstan Ranfurly Kyeburn Herbert
Bungy Jumping Omakau
Remarkables Ophir Poolburn Waipiata Kokonga KAKANUI
Skifield Clyde Chatto Moa Creek Morrisons MOUNTAINS Hampden
Creek Patearoa Moeraki Boulders
Earnscleugh Macraes Flat Dunback Moeraki
Kingston Fruitlands Alexandra Poolburn Katiki Point
Kingston Flyer Manorburn Reservoir
(Train) Reservoir
Fairlight North Mavora Greenland
nau Downs Lake Reservoir

TRANZ ALPINE TRAIN

The gentle clackety-clack of track against wheel beats a soothing soulful rhythm as passengers relax and enjoy a panorama of vibrant colour and sparkling contrast. Deep gorges whiz by, with glimpses of clear mountain water rushing through wide shingle riverbeds below. Dark-green broom forms a rich backdrop to shaggy cinnamon-brown tussock, while snow-frosted mountains of all shapes and sizes are dramatic bystanders in every scene.

It's just another clear sunny day on TranzAlpine, rated as one of the world's top six scenic train journeys, and an unforgettable way to traverse the Southern Alps from Christchurch to Greymouth.

The TranzAlpine rail journey is 231 kilometres long and it takes four and a half-hours to travel one way. There's plenty of excitement both there and back with 16 rather close-fitting tunnels, and an open air viewing carriage allowing passengers to get even closer to the stunning scenery as well as providing fantastic photo opportunities at key points en route. Most carriages hold a maximum of 50 people and include both one-way seating and tabled group seating allowing passengers to experience the amazing views whilst enjoying the company of others.

The TranzAlpine departs at 8.15 am daily from the Christchurch Railway Station on Troupe Drive, off Clarence Street in Addington. To take advantage of their limited number of Super-Saver fares, Train Tickets Online recommend booking as far in advance as possible.

The TranzAlpine's onboard "Snacks on Tracks" menu offers some hearty favourites including Shepherds Pie, Baked Potatoes, Chicken Coconut Coriander Curry and delicious hot bacon and egg rolls. Coffee, tea, muffins, fruit salad and Devonshire teas are also available, as are beer and wine.

An informative and entertaining commentary, a unique blend of local history, folklore and legend, is provided throughout the trip.

Warm clothes are required for the open viewing carriage – even during the summer – and in the winter a jacket and gloves are recommended for outdoor wear.

For further information please visit www.traintickets.co.nz or from within NZ phone 0800 500 660. From outside NZ dial +64 3 379 1451.

Train Tickets Online is an authorised agent of Tranz Scenic.

An hour after departure a stop is made at Springfield, where more passengers are collected before the TranzAlpine continues on, leaving the productive farmland and fields of the Canterbury Plains behind and climbing through the foothills of the Southern Alps, through the spectacular gorges and river valleys of the Waimakariri River. Another stop is made at Arthur's Pass, where time is allowed to stretch your legs and take photos of this quaint alpine village, 737 metres above sea level.

Then the whistle sounds and the train departs, winding its way through majestic mountains before slowly descending through lush beech rainforest to Greymouth, the largest town on the West Coast.

Established beside the mouth of the Grey River and built on an old gold mining site, Greymouth has an interesting history and it is well worth visiting the local museum.

One hour is provided to explore the museum and some of the town's arts and crafts stores including greenstone sculptures, gold jewellery, hand knits and pottery, before reboarding the TranzAlpine for the return trip to Christchurch. ■

When one thinks of the West Coast, visions of rugged and dramatic hills, acres of rainforest and spectacular surf spring to mind, but from Greymouth to Westport the scenery also has an almost tropical appeal with nikau palms sprouting from glistening white sands and clinging to rocky escarpments. In Punakaiki, a friendly holiday town made famous by its stunning pancake rocks, salty spray flies from blowholes, while nearby Westport, a town often overlooked, provides many unique activities for the intrepid traveller. Inland, avid anglers have the opportunity to try their luck on the internationally renowned waters of the Murchison/Nelson Lakes region, where some of the best fly fishing in NZ can be found on Lake Rotoroa, Lake Rotoiti, and up the Travers, D'Urville and Sabine Rivers.

We spend three days driving the scenic route from Greymouth to Nelson. We visit a world renowned pounamu (jade) sculptor, admire Punakaiki's pancake rocks, ride rapids aboard jet skis in Westport, enjoy indigenous cuisine, join a thrilling whitewater rafting expedition down the mighty Buller River, and angle for elusive brown trout!

GREYMOUTH TO NELSON

DAY ONE
Greymouth to Westport, via Punakaiki

Overnight Bob's been doing his research on the famous pancake rocks in Punakaiki and he's keen to get on the road. But first we call into the acclaimed Jade Boulder Gallery, a museum that tells the story of this precious stone, known to the Maori as pounamu. There's lots to see including a range of unique sculpture and jewellery designed and hand-crafted by Ian Boustridge and his team of master carvers; some of the pieces took over a year to design and sculpt. At the entrance we marvel over a five-ton jade boulder – the largest to be recovered in the Southern Hemisphere. Bob places his hands on its smooth, cool surface like an alternative healer extracting its energy and then we meet Ian (named as one of the top five jade sculptors in the world by the National Geographic Society) in his studio where he's busy working on a new piece.

"I guess my passion for jade began when I was about 17 years old," Ian tells us, "I used to collect the stone and carve it in my grandmother's chook-house." Today, some thirty years later, collectors worldwide covet his work.

We drive north to Rapahoe where the road joins the coast and offers fabulous views of rugged hills, dramatic headlands and rolling surf. From Barrytown the landscape changes: coastal plains dotted with nikau palms are flanked by bush-clad hills.

More palms cling obstinately to the layered rock escarpments in Punakaiki, creating a tropical backdrop to the green-blue sea. "It's got a Hawaiian feel!" says Bob as we park the car and walk the Dept. of Conservation track to the blowholes at Punakaiki's famous pancake rocks. The timing couldn't be more perfect: it's high tide and there's a good ocean swell so salt-laden spray is flying. Bob gets some great shots and then after lunch at Punakaiki Tavern we walk along the beach and collect pieces of perfectly polished, pure-white quartz.

There are several good hikes in the area including the Pororari River Track, the Truman Track, Fox River Cave Walk, Cave Creek/Kotihotiho Walk and the Punakaiki-Pororari Loop, but our legs have been stretched, and so we continue north. On the outskirts of Punakaiki we visit the Te Miko Glass Bead Studio, where we watch Carolyn Hewlett as she crafts each individual flame-worked bead, before we drive to Westport and join a unique jet-ski tour with Xtreme Adventures on the lower reaches of the Buller River.

After donning wetsuits our small group gets a safety rundown and quick basic lesson from guide Steve Reynolds then we're off, charging up the river behind Steve. At first it's pretty

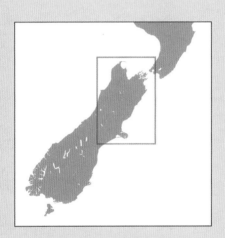

mellow and there's plenty of time to practise our manoeuvres. Bob rides companionably by my side for a short time, then drops back to jump my wake. Then we swap over. It's loads of fun and just as we think it can't get any better we hit the rapids, flying off the back of one wave then hitting another. Seventy kilometres later we return, exhilarated, to Westport. After checking into our accommodation and enjoying hot showers, we drive to Tauranga Bay (near Cape Foulwind) for a late afternoon stroll to the seal colony.

As the sun begins to set our mighty appetites lead us to Tauranga Bay's acclaimed Bay Café. Here we discover a modern NZ menu featuring some of the country's finest fare from squid stuffed with kumara and coconut served with a sweet curry sauce, to caramelized passion-fruit and lemon tart. "Oh what to choose," sighs Bob as we relax and peruse the menu at a candle-lit window table overlooking the bay. In the end he decides upon one of chef Luke Macann's past entries into the Monteiths' Wild Food Challenge, 'All clammed up and nowhere to go'. "Unbelievably tasty," Bob says later, swallowing his last morsel of this indigenous ragout of shellfish accompanied by Tauranga Bay seaweed salad, tua tua wontons, and horopito and watercress purée. "I would never have believed wild foods could taste this good!"

DAY TWO
Westport to Murchison

In the morning the feasting continues with a hearty breakfast in town before we visit Coaltown, a museum that brings Westport's history alive through its sawmilling, gold and coal mining, and shipping displays. We spend an hour looking around and then leave town on SH6 following the Buller River inland to Inangahua Junction, then on through the Upper Buller Gorge Scenic Reserve to Newton Flat where, shortly after, we stop at the 110 metre long swingbridge over the raging Buller Gorge. We enjoy a latté then cross the wobbling bridge to the other side, where we decide to ride the comet line, a 160 metre long flying fox, back across the river. It's a blast; but Bob's slightly vertiginous, and yells all the way!

After a lunch of egg and cucumber sandwiches in nearby Murchison, a small town that offers a range of high adrenaline activities – most of which centre on or around the river – we don wetsuits at Ultimate Descents and join a whitewater rafting tour. Bob's a little hesitant, he's not sure what to expect, but after we board our raft and receive expert instruction from Dean, our whitewater rafting guide, he begins to visibly relax.

The first stretch of river is tame - great for first-timers. I slip into a quiet reverie as our raft drifts along the Buller's crystal clear waters; a kaleidoscope of colours reflect from the surrounding hills onto the river's glassy surface and beneath lies a riverbed of perfectly polished pebbles.

"F-O-R-WARD!" Dean's bellowed commands suddenly shatter the silence. "LEFT! RIGHT! F-O-R-W-A-R-D!" Bob shoots me a horrified look as our raft gathers momentum, sweeps around a bend, and we come face to face with a tumbling tower of bottle-green waves and foaming white wash. For a precarious moment we perch at the crest of the towering wall, then we're at right angles descending into the roaring foam.

Greymouth to Nelson:
Attractions and Activities

Jade Boulder Gallery: www.jadeboulder.com
Pancake Rocks: Punakaiki
Te Miko Glass Bead Studio: Punakaiki
Xtreme Adventures: www.xtremeadventures.co.nz
Coaltown: Westport
Buller Swingbridge: www.bullergorge.co.nz
Ultimate Descents: www.rivers.co.nz
Trout Fishing: www.guidedflyfishingnz.com
Water Taxi: www.starnaud.co.nz
Troutwise Women: www.starnaud.co.nz/activities.htm

Greymouth to Nelson:
Cafés and Eateries

The Bay Café: Tauranga Bay, Westport
Wild Coast Café: 4300 Coast Rd, Punakaiki
Rivers Café: 51 Fairfax St, Murchison
Elaine's Alpine Café: Main Rd, St Arnaud
Tophouse: Tophouse Rd, St Arnaud
The Naked Bun: 66 Aranui Rd, Mapua
Smokehouse Café: Wharf Shed 3, Mapua

> Our raft gathers momentum, sweeps around a bend, and we come face to face with a tumbling tower of bottle-green waves and foaming white wash

The last thing I see before the world turns abruptly white is Bob's grimly determined expression.

Through the white-out Dean can be heard shouting at us to hold on. Between gasping and screaming there's no time for communication at our end of the raft!

Seconds later we emerge from the rushing icy whiteness only to charge headlong into another rapid. Adrenaline kicks in and we're loving it. Eventually we emerge at the other end - totally unscathed. "That was amazing," says Bob later, as we're checking into a farm stay on the outskirts of Murchison. Then he gives me a strange expression, "You know I'm positive I came face to face with a trout!"

DAY THREE
Murchison to Nelson

After his fishy encounter on the Ariki Falls, Bob decides a spot of fly fishing is in order today. Fortunately we're in precisely the right place for the trout fishing at Lakes Rotoroa and Rotoiti, and up the D'Urville,

Sabine and Travers Rivers is internationally renowned.

We drive to beautiful Lake Rotoroa nestled against the mountainous backdrop of the Nelson Lakes National Park and while Bob shoots off with local fishing guide, Russell Frost, I hike up the beginning of the Porika track, a rocky zigzagging four-wheel drive route, with excellent lake and mountain views.

Then, as I'm not expecting Bob to return until noon, I hike a short way along the lakeside track, a rough path through podocarp and beech forest which skirts around the eastern shoreline of the lake to Sabine Hut, before doubling back to meet Bob at the car.

He's had an "awesome" morning stalking brown trout and tells me all about it as we drive to the village of St. Arnaud, where we stop for a late lunch at Tophouse, an historic cob (mud) cottage which dates back to the 1880s. Back in its early days the lodge was frequented by drovers transporting sheep through the valley and onto the Marlborough and the Canterbury plains.

After seeing the bullet holes in the verandah (left after a double murder/suicide in 1894), and perusing the range of local arts and crafts housed in what was once NZ's smallest bar, we drive down to the lake and hop aboard Bill Butters' water taxi service. His service is used by trampers hiking the four to seven day Travers-Sabine circuit or completing day hikes such as the Lake Rotoiti Circuit, the Mount Robert loop track, the St Arnaud Range track, and the Whisky Falls track.

Others, like us, hire his services for a scenic tour of the lake. A local born and bred (his family has lived here since the 1860s), Bill tells us he moved back here in '85 for a lifestyle change. On the far side of the lake he shows us the breathtaking Whisky Falls and at the lake head the water is so clear that we can see trout undulating in the current. On the return Bob tells Bill all about his morning fly fishing excursion. "What did you do?" Bill asks me. When he discovers that I've never hooked a trout before he gets excited. "My wife Betty can teach you!" he exclaims.

Bob's so keen that I too experience the pleasure of trout fishing that he shouts me the lesson and before I know it, Betty's down on the

Punakaiki Rocks - Deerace Publishing

shore and I'm booked into a two-hour "Troutwise Women" course. Bob takes off to the Dept. of Conservation visitor centre to view its displays, then hikes through beech forests dripping with honeydew and swarming with bellbirds in the Rotoiti Nature Recovery Project, while I head off with Betty for my first fly fishing lesson.

To begin with Betty shows me classic trout tucker – live nymphs, then I'm taught how to prepare my rod with a weight forward floating fly line and a nymphing rig. The rig has a small artificial nymph on the bottom, a weighted nymph above and a strike indicator attached so I can easily identify a strike.

Next up is tension casting. "Look where you're aiming," Betty instructs as I cast the line. Once this is mastered I then learn to mend the line; a key part of the lesson. "If you don't mend properly it won't matter how good your casting is, the nymph will look unnatural as it floats through the water and the trout will ignore it," says Betty.

Mending the line proves difficult, but after a lot of practice my nymph is moving through the water in a natural drag-free drift and Betty says I'm ready to fool a wily old trout. She leaves me to play while she pours us a thermos tea and suddenly my indicator disappears. It's a strike!

I yank the rod upwards and holler for help.

Betty comes running with the net and I jump up and down like a six-year-old catching her first sprat.

"How'd it go?" asks Bob later when we triumphantly return. "Magic," I say as I load my six-pounder carefully into the chilly-bin (much to Bob's horror as he's strictly a tag and release kind of guy). We wave goodbye to Bill and Betty as we leave town and head north to Richmond. Then, instead of driving into the city, I indicate for Ruby Bay.

"If we're staying in Nelson," says Bob, consulting the map, "We're going the wrong way!"

"Oh – sorry – change of plan," I reply, "I thought we'd stay at Clayridge instead."

"Why the sudden change?" asks Bob in a puzzled tone.

"W-e-ll – it's got fabulous rooms, great views, a good breakfast... oh yes and then there's the broadband..." I end lamely.

Bob shoots me a quizzical look.

"OK, I'm sprung," I admit impatiently, "but we've got a trout on ice in need of a good smoking and Clayridge is closer to the Smokehouse Café!" ▪

The South Island is the island of action and adventure and here where the northern tip of the Southern Alps meets the Murchison/Nelson Lakes region visitors have two choices: relax and soak up the beautiful scenery, or break personal boundaries and enjoy a new activity in the great outdoors.

And from snow sports such as skiing, snow-boarding and ice-skating; to mountain biking; jet boating; kayaking; fly fishing; or even cometing – an activity unique to this region – there's no lack of adrenaline pumping activities to choose from!

During the winter the Rainbow Ski Field near St Arnaud provides a range of skiing and boarding trails for the novice through to the more advanced. Access to the top of the range is provided by chairlifts, while skiers at Mt Robert Ski Field must take a stiff two hour hike up the aptly named Pinchgut track to the slopes, or catch a ride in a helicopter for around $40.

However it's the year-round whitewater rafting and kayaking opportunities that provide the greatest drawcard to the region. Murchison is fast earning a reputation as the kayaking capital of NZ as it has a wide range of accessible paddling on offer from steep creeks to big volume rivers and runs. Reliable river flows ensure excellent paddling year-round and the region is becoming a popular destination for experienced international paddlers.

Ultimate Descents offer kayak expeditions ex-Murchison for first-timers aboard inflatable or sit-upon kayaks and no previous experience is necessary. The guaranteed ratio of one guide to every four paddlers ensures everyone gets the most out of their kayaking experience.

Murchison is also the base for The New Zealand Kayak School which runs residential kayak courses for beginners, intermediate and advanced paddlers, with coaching provided by some of NZ's top professional instructors.

MURCHISON ACTION

The crystal-clear upper reaches of the mighty Buller River provide some of the best stretches of white water in NZ. There are plenty of thrills and spills for both first timers and experienced paddlers alike.

Whitewater rafting expeditions with tour operators such as Ultimate Descents depart daily from Murchison. The awe inspiring journey down the Buller River begins with a float on peaceful waters where the only sounds are the gurgling current and the rhythmic splash of paddles slicing through the water. There's plenty of time for each whitewater rafting crew member to get a good grip on their paddle before hitting the big stuff: the granite canyons where roaring white water carves its way through deep gorges. The training certainly pays off when the raft is perched precariously at the crest of a towering bottle-green wave, about to take an 80-degree dive down into foaming whitewash! All this action is spiced up even more with challenging waterfalls such as Ariki, a formidable fall dubbed Freaky Ariki by the locals!

As well as adrenaline-pumping water sports the local rivers also provide excellent fly fishing opportunities. Lake Rotoroa and Lake Rotoiti are internationally renowned for fly fishing and many visitors choose to hire guides who know the region well. On the upper reaches of the Buller River visitors can enjoy the challenge of stalking brown trout in waters so clear you can see them – and they can see you, which makes it a real hunting experience.

During the summer months jet boating on the Buller is an option, and at the 'Swingbridge' over the raging Buller Gorge, cometing provides a whole new way to get across! A word of caution however: if you find the 110-metre long swingbridge challenging, don't even consider a comet ride as you will find yourself strapped in, tied up and swinging like a puppet at the end of string, ready to fly off the platform across the gorge in no time at all!

Not quite so 'on the edge' is the comet line, a 160-metre flying fox with a seat. But those who do make it across the river in one piece whatever their mode of transport can try their luck panning for gold or stroll along the banks of the Buller to Ariki Falls and the Whites Creek faultline, the site of the 1929 Murchison earthquake. ■

A wise man once said that when you drive over the Takaka Hill, you leave all your troubles behind. In Takaka, the gateway to Golden Bay, this certainly seems to be true for here life moves to a relaxed and friendly beat, and its locals, many of whom are creative artisans, endorse strong environmental principles. In nearby Collingwood, where there are "no strangers only friends never met", the end of the road draws nigh. Here where the mountainous Wakamarama and Burnett Ranges roll down to meet the blue-green horseshoe of Golden Bay, the world's longest spit of sand curves into Cook Strait like an overgrown talon. Farewell Spit is one of NZ's most important bird sanctuaries; here amongst the shifting dunes and indigenous grasses, over 90 species of native and migratory birds make their home. We spend three days exploring this unique 'cul-de-sac'. We visit local artists and shop in boutique stores, hike in the Abel Tasman National Park, fish for salmon, visit the world's clearest springs, gorge ourselves silly on 'Rosy Glow' chocolates, and take a four wheel drive tour up Farewell Spit to spy on native and migratory birds.

NELSON TO
GOLDEN BAY

DAY ONE
Nelson to Takaka

As we pass through the small beachside settlements of Tasman Bay and on to Motueka, it's clear to Bob and I that creative folk – artists, potters, sculptors, weavers, carvers, photographers and poets – abound in these parts. We pass several small boutiques, galleries and studios displaying unique wares, as well as simple roadside stalls where excess homegrown produce is sold.

Orchards of apples and hops sweep by as we begin the steep drive up Takaka Hill, passing Ngarua Caves to reach the top where we're offered fabulous views of the Anatoki Range and flat coastal plains below.

We take a drive by Takaka's collection of quirky cafes, then hike through the craggy limestone outcrops of the Grove Scenic Reserve in Clifton, where native trees and ferns cling precariously to the top.

Bob (ever mindful of his stomach) spots a sign for Golden Salami and so we follow the signs to Alan Climpson's Sussex beef farm where all the salami is handmade from meat produced by their own cows. It's mixed with herbs, spices, salt, sugar and brandy then cured slowly, European-style, to produce a tangy flavour.

After selecting a salami to join the fruits and crackers already in our picnic basket, we continue on our way. At the Wainui Falls, a 30 minute hike brings us to a swing bridge with an impressive view of the thundering water. We enjoy a cup of thermos coffee on a large boulder in the sun then hike back down the trail to continue our drive through dense forest to the ochre-tinted sands of Totaranui in the Abel Tasman National Park.

"Let's go somewhere quiet to picnic," suggests Bob, in contemplative mood after the waterfall experience. Information on all the hikes – which range from 20-minutes to five days – is provided in the Dept. of Conservation office. We choose the one-hour Coast Track to Anapai Bay which journeys over the headland and when we arrive we have the beach all to ourselves. After a refreshing dip in the warm ocean, we eat our tasty salami-based picnic and laze in the sun before returning to Totaranui, where - much to Bob's delight - I suggest we go salmon fishing.

We drive back to Takaka then head to Anatoki Salmon, a fresh water salmon farm located in a sheltered valley beside the Anatoki River.

You can buy direct from the farm, or fish to your heart's content, paying only for your catch. As we only need one fish we share the rod but it's Bob who pulls in a beautiful 3.4 kilo

fish which is then efficiently weighed, gutted and gilled, and placed on ice in a polystyrene container for easy transportation. There's a BBQ and smoking facilities onsite but we opt instead to head straight to our accommodation at Sans Souci Inn, an eco-friendly lodge near the beach. When we arrive our friendly hosts, Vera and Reto Balzer whisk our salmon into their manuka smoker.

After settling into our rooms we explore the inn, it's housed in a long, circular mudbrick building with clay tiles, turf insulated ceilings, and spotless, sweet-scented composting toilets, then we join other guests and relax in a cobbled courtyard amid lush, tropical plantings. After a delicious dinner of delectable smoked salmon, we find that Sans Souci's eco-friendly ways are quite a talking point amongst guests, many of whom are outdoorsy types and keen environmentalists. Bob, intrigued by the inn's unique bathrooms, quizzes Reto about the composting process until late in the evening – discovering, amongst other facts, that it takes around two years to produce a safe, organic fertiliser.

"Well then," I hear Bob saying to Reto as I slip quietly off to my room, "Why on earth aren't we all composting?"

DAY TWO
Takaka to Collingwood

In the morning we enjoy a light breakfast before taking a leisurely stroll around the friendly township of Takaka, perusing its array of quirky craft studios and galleries, and small boutique village stores, before driving to the Waikoropupu Springs, the clearest freshwater springs in the world.

"Wow," says Bob, gazing at the iridescent blue and green springs which sparkle like polished paua, "They're beautiful!" The springs rise through thick layers of marbled rock and discharge around 14,000 litres of water per second. We hike around the edge of the pools passing water milfoil, forget-me-nots and rushes on a track that leads to various viewing platforms. There are several informative display boards en route and we learn that the springs are home to freshwater snails, long finned eels and koura (freshwater crayfish). "Look," says Bob, "they were once used by the Maori for ceremonial blessings."

We spend time soaking up the peaceful atmosphere then drive through the countryside to the Mussel Inn Bush Café, a country pub selling local food and drink. We join others on the wide, shady verandah screened by vines of hops, and relish every mouthful of the thick mussel chowder we're served, washing it down with an organic beer that is brewed onsite.

Bob pops inside to settle our account and returns with an amazed look on his face, "There's a bounty for possum tails," he says incredulously, obviously recalling all the squashed possums we've seen on the road during our circumnavigation of NZ. "Every tail earns a pint on the house and if you bring in a rat's tail, you'll get a chocolate fish!"

Bob marvels at the locals' endorsement of strong environmental principles all the way to Tukurua, where we leave State Highway 60 and follow a back street lined with roadside stalls. We stop to admire pottery at Flax Gully and fragrant handcrafted candles at Living Light Candles,

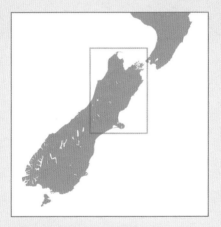

Nelson-Golden Bay Area:
Attractions and Activities

Farewell Spit Safari: www.farewellspit.co.nz
Cape Farewell Horse Treks: www.horsetreksnz.com
Golden Bay Kayaks: www.goldenbaykayaks.co.nz
Kahurangi Guided Walks: www.kahurangiwalks.co.nz
Waikoropupu Springs: Takaka
Anatoki Salmon Farm: www.anatokisalmon.co.nz
Ngarua Caves: Takaka
Abel Tasman Kayaks: www.abeltasmankayaks.co.nz
Nelson Wine and Arts Trail: www.nelsonwines.co.nz
Te Anaroa Caves: Rockwell, Collingwood

Nelson-Golden Bay Area:
Cafés and Eateries

Courthouse Café and Gallery: Haven Rd, Collingwood
Mussel Inn: Onekaka, Takaka
Penguin Café and Bar: Abel Tasman Drive, Pohara
Wholemeal Café: Commercial St, Takaka
Dangerous Kitchen: Commercial St, Takaka
Bencari Farm and Café: Takaka
Old School Café: Pakawau, Collingwood

> "We join others on the wide, shady verandah screened by vines of hops, and relish every mouthful of the thick mussel chowder"

before driving to the beach where we step upon aureate sands to delight in the sparkling arch of Golden Bay.

Then we continue on to Collingwood and check into a local B&B. Later, at our host's suggestion, we climb the hill to St Cuthbert's, a tiny Anglican church built in 1873 for a bird's eye view of this tiny town. Below, the 1905 Courthouse - now a popular café - buzzes with patrons and a steady stream of visitors stop to inspect the historic displays housed in the town's tiny museum.

After booking a place aboard Paddy Gillooly's famous Original Farewell Spit Safari for the following morning, we pay a visit to Rosy Glow Chocolates. Here we find a delicious array of handcrafted confectionery and after choosing a (rather large) selection we drive inland to Rockville's Te Anaroa Caves, munching on chocolates as we go.

At the caves we join a half hour guided tour to see its highlights, including beautiful bacon drapes, straws and columns, as well as fossilised scallop shells, gypsum flowers and penguin bones. Bob even spots a signature by WD Lash dating back to 1884.

When we emerge the light is beginning to fade and so we return to

the Courthouse Café in Collingwood where where we have a dinner of fresh panfried groper with a roasted red pepper and basil sauce, before turning in.

DAY THREE
Farewell Spit

The morning dawns bright and clear for our guided expedition up Farewell Spit and we board a unique 4wd bus, which has tiered seating to guarantee everyone a good view.

En route our guide for the morning, Kersten Franke, provides a brief history of the local region from coal mining in Puponga to the Aorere goldrush of 1857, then tells us that Farewell Spit began life 6,500 years ago and lengthens by six and a half metres every year. "It's a fragile ecosystem, so no public vehicle access is permitted," he says, "and only four kilometres of its 35 km length may be seen on foot."

While the Tasman Sea pounds Farewell Spit's northern coast, its sheltered southern shores provide a safe haven for shellfish and waders. On this inner beach we spot many natives: white herons, South Island pied oyster catchers, banded dotterels and Caspian terns. As we cross the dunes to the Tasman Sea the migratory birds come out to play. There's the Turnstone, an inquisitive bird busily examining stranded debris, who will soon be off to the Northern Hemisphere to breed on the Arctic Coast, and throngs of Eastern Bar-tailed Godwits preparing for their journey to North-eastern Siberia. "How on earth do they find the spit when they return here every year," Bob wonders aloud.

It's 27 km to the lighthouse along a route that the Original Farewell Spit Safari team knows well as in 1946 they began a mail run to the lighthouse, transporting supplies to the keepers and their families. "Visitors came along for the ride and so the tours began," Kersten tells us as we disembark to look at crescent-shaped dunes rising high above blackened salt pans, before journeying on to the semi-arid surrounds of the lighthouse.

The first lighthouse was built in 1870 from jarrah, an Australian

hardwood, but it was blasted to pieces by the sand so a new steel tower was built in 1897. Inside, over morning tea, we peruse the historical photos plastered all over its walls. "Look here," says Bob, pointing at a map from 1945 which depicts how fast the spit is growing, "The gannets' nests didn't exist back then."

We climb aboard the bus and continue up the beach, past scattered driftwood and basking seals to the gannets' nesting site. "Amazing," says Bob, zooming in with his camera to watch as their smoky-grey young flap their wings in preparation for their inaugural flight.

Later we return by bus to Collingwood to collect the car, then enjoy a late lunch at the Old School Café and Bar in the sleepy seaside village of Pakawau. Earlier in the morning Bob noted the site of another lighthouse, Pillar Point, set high on the rocky outcrops of the Old Man Range. He's keen to take a look because he says there will be fabulous views of the spit.

We pass through Puponga where the poles from the old jetty begin to protrude as the tide goes out, and shortly afterwards the road ends at Puponga Farm Park, a strip of land created by the government to form a protection belt around Farewell Spit.

An information centre provides details on local hikes including the 20-minute walk to Wharariki Beach with its spectacular jumble of caves,

islets, rock pools and sand dunes; Cape Farewell, where Captain Cook said goodbye when he left NZ in 1770; and the Old Man Range and Pillar Point Lighthouse, dubbed 'blinking billy' by the locals, which is also the site of NZ's first radar station, used during WW2.

Feeling too lazy to hike we decide instead to ride up with Gail McKnight of Cape Farewell Horse Treks. She assures us that it's a good easy ride for beginners. "Wharariki Beach is great for advanced riders, they can open up out there," she says, as I board Bungle, a sprightly cod-liver chestnut with a dark mane and tail. Bob's riding a beautiful dark horse whom he insists calling Black Beauty all the way to the top of the range where we're greeted by absolutely stunning views, a full 360 sweep from Farewell Spit through to Abel Tasman National Park. It's such a clear day that even the silhouette of Mt Taranaki can be seen vaguely on the horizon. "It's an awesome backyard," says Gail looking around at us and smiling. "I never grow tired of coming up here."

Bob snaps merrily away with his camera as the sun begins to drop on the horizon casting a golden glow on the wet sand flats below. Suddenly he jerks up from his camera and waves me over to his side. "Look," he says incredulously, pointing to Farewell Spit which curves in a glorious golden band below, "It's just like a kiwi's beak – that's how the migratory birds know they've arrived home!" ∎

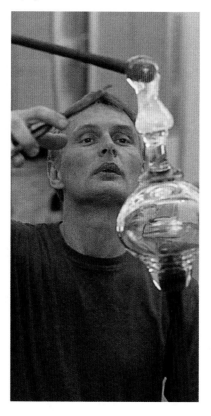

The Nelson region embraces creativity and design, and is renowned throughout New Zealand for its wealth of talented artisans and art-loving individuals. Painters, potters, sculptors, weavers, glass artists, wood turners, weavers, carvers, jewellers, furniture-makers, and so the list goes on, have made their home here by the sea, forming and becoming part of the creative landscape.

The region revels in its artistic make-up, supporting up-and-coming artists and celebrating its creative spirit with various arts and music festivals, held throughout the year.

The largest ever conceived in this region was the Montana WearableArt (WOW) Awards, where art is taken off the wall and used to adorn the body in wildly wonderful (and somewhat wacky!) ways. It was the brainchild of local sculptor Suzie Moncrieff in 1987 and the first show which had 50 entries, was held in a large tent.

Today the production is a major annual event and although the show itself is now staged in Wellington, Nelson was its birthplace and this is celebrated at the World of WearableArt and Collectable Cars Museum. It's located near the airport, making it the perfect first or last stop on the Nelson arts trail for those flying in or out of the city.

Inside this aesthetically pleasing architecturally designed building there are two main galleries to view. One houses collectable cars while the other is dedicated to wearable art and showcases creatively displayed garments from the annual awards show, housed in a unique gallery using theatrical lighting, movement and music. This gallery also includes an ultra-violet room where the Illumination Illusion section of the show can be experienced. Next door an audiovisual presentation tells the story of WOW and features dramatic excerpts from the show. Local paintings can be viewed and purchased from the Reflections Gallery and a retail shop provides a glimpse into the works of local clothing, jewellery and ceramics artists.

NELSON ARTS

In the city, The Suter Te Aratoi o Whakatu, the public art museum for the Nelson region is central to the locals love of art, for here a substantial collection of NZ artworks has been exhibited for more than 100 years. The Suter's collection includes paintings by CF Goldie, DK Richmond, Mina Arndt, Frances Hodgkins, Philip Clairmont, Jane Evans, Tony Fomison, Austin Davies and Sally Burton.

The city also boasts a variety of modern boutique artisan stores which showcase local Nelson artworks including Element Gallery, Shine, South Street Gallery, Jewel Beetle, Rome, Catastrophe and Catchment Gallery – just to name a few! Element Gallery and Books is located at the Nelson Visitor Information Centre on the corner of Trafalgar and Halifax Streets and is an excellent starting point for viewing the very best of Nelson Art and New Zealand books.

And with more working artists in Nelson, per capita, than anywhere else in NZ, it's not hard to find them hard at work in their home studios or galleries! For many, a telephone appointment should first be made and the Nelson Guide Book, Art in its Own Place provides a comprehensive guide with a complete listing of artists' works, phone numbers and addresses. At centres such as the Grape Escape Complex in Richmond which incorporates a café, art and craft gallery, Living Light Candles gallery and workshop, Prenzels Liqueurs tasting room and cellar door for two quality Nelson wines – Te Mania and the organic, Richmond Plains – a variety of local and regional arts can be viewed, while the Coolstore Gallery on Mapua Wharf is one of the region's funkiest galleries and showcases the works of more than 60 established and emerging artists.

At the Höglund Art Glass International Glass Centre, an informative guided tour of the facility's glass gallery, store, museum and glassblowing studio, departs daily at 1.30 pm. Here husband and wife team, glass artists Ola Höglund and Marie Simberg-Höglund design and produce their unique handblown art glass using several complex glassblowing techniques including Graal, Ariel and Incalmo.

Watching glassblowers as they work is a riveting business. Ola describes the work of a glassblower as being a bit like a musician – every day is spent practising and training. "As an artist I am fascinated by making a form with the human breath," he says, "the heat of the furnace and the molten, soft glass are my inspiration."

Those who think it looks easy will soon realise their error if they enrol on one of the Höglund's popular courses – glass bead making, paperweight making or lampworks. Classes are held throughout the year and no previous experience is necessary. ▪

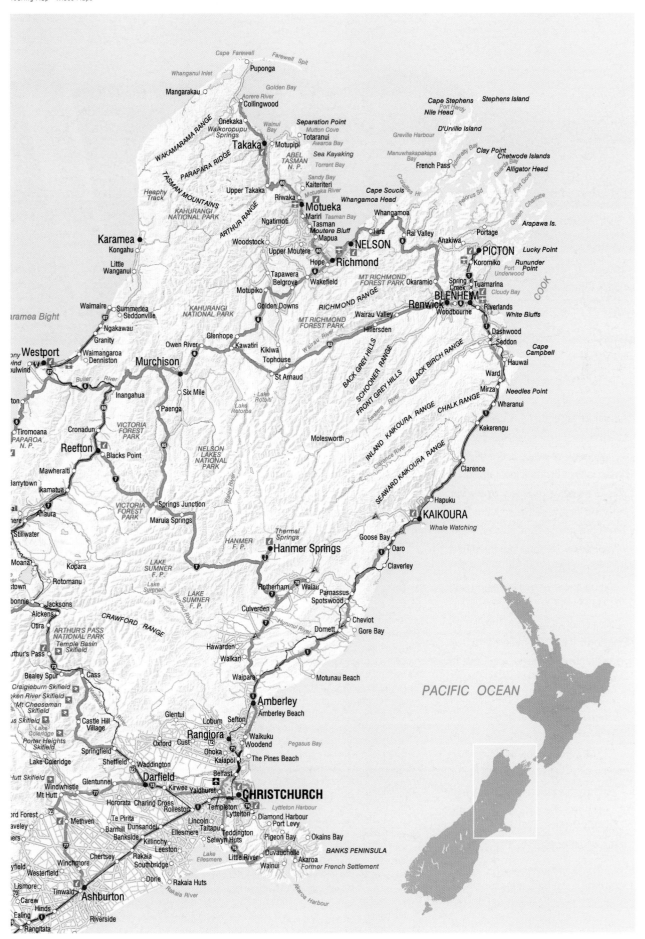

PACIFIC OCEAN

The Marlborough Sounds: New Zealand just doesn't come any cleaner or greener. Its waters are so pure that many of these spectacular sunken sea valleys are used to commercially cultivate a local delicacy, NZ Greenshell mussels. With over 1500 kilometres of coastline the Marlborough Sounds also provides a pristine environment to enjoy a number of sea-based activities from sailing and diving to kayaking and fishing. A popular way to explore the region is by hiking the Queen Charlotte Track, a 71 kilometre trail leading from historic Ship Cove to Anakiwa. It provides breathtaking views of the Queen Charlotte and Kenepuru Sounds en route, and is open to mountain bikers from March through to November.

On the final leg of our circumnavigation of NZ, Bob and I spend two days exploring the Marlborough Sounds. We dine on Greenshell Mussels, take a Mussel cruise, catch a water taxi to an isolated lodge where we have a feast of fresh seafood, then journey on to Picton where we say our final farewells.

NELSON TO **PICTON**

DAY ONE
Nelson to Kenepuru Sound via Havelock

It's 10 am and Bob and I are dragging our tails. Somehow it's hard to believe that we're about to embark on the last sector of what has been an incredible scenic drive around NZ.

Bob finishes packing the boot and then we're off, following SH6 along the coast before turning inland to Hira and the Rai Valley. "It's an absolute shambles back there," says Bob, pointing towards the boot, "I need some time to sort it all out."

I nod, wondering what on earth he intends to do with all the paraphernalia he's collected throughout our travels, let alone how he intends to transport his burgeoning boot-cellar!

We cross the one-way bridge over the Pelorus River and stop for a latté at the Pelorus Bridge Café in the scenic reserve by the river. There's a delicious selection of homemade pies: chicken and camembert, venison, and wild pork with apple and kumara. Bob eyes them hungrily but we continue on to Havelock where a relaxed holiday-like air permeates. We park outside Creative Flair, a gallery displaying local arts and crafts including incredible paintings of the sea by Rick Edmonds. Bob's totally captivated by them. He buys a print and rolls it in a tube for easy transportation.

Then we take a seat at Mussel Boys. I enjoy a large bowl of Mussel Boys' Chowder, while Bob tucks into a pot of steamers, fresh mussels whole in their shell. He takes the first mussel out with his fingers, then uses the shell like a pair of tweezers to extract the other mussels in true Mussel Boy style, as shown on a chart on the wall. Then, looking rather sheepish, he orders some flats, fresh whole mussels grilled on half a shell. "Piggy," I say, laughing.

After lunch we hop aboard the Greenshell Mussel Cruise, a unique wine and food tour that cruises the inner Pelorus and the tranquil Kenepuru Sounds. Once aboard we learn the history of the sounds and the history of the local people, then visit a Greenshell mussel farm where we're shown how mussels are commercially cultivated on longlines.

We tour several idyllic bays and coves and there's the opportunity to match mussels with local wines (which Bob adores); amongst other facts we learn that each mussel is capable of filtering about 300 litres of water a day!

"That's a lot of water," says Bob, as we cruise back into the marina at Havelock.

Back in the car we leave SH6 in favour of scenic Queen Charlotte Drive. As we leave town we're offered fantastic views back down over Havelock before we continue on to Linkwater, where we turn off for Te Mahia. The route takes us about 30 minutes, even though it only looks like a short distance on the map. Here we abandon our trusty rental and gathering our overnight gear, climb aboard a water taxi for the trip across the Kenepuru Sound to Hopewell.

Primarily it's a relaxed upmarket backpackers' lodge but it has a secret: there's one newly renovated and self-contained two bedroom cottage right on the waters edge, and this will be our home for the night.

We've come prepared with basic food supplies for there are no shops in these parts: rice, chilli, onion, garlic, tinned tomatoes, and bacon and eggs with a crusty loaf for breakfast. Oh, and a few

bottles of Marlborough wine.

There are several single and two-seater kayaks available for guests' use, but Bob borrows a dinghy and some fishing gear (all free of charge) and rows into the sound while I gather sizeable mussels and oysters from the rocks nearby.

Some time later Bob returns grinning with a decent snapper and, acting the goat, sticks a white paper bag on his head like a chef's hat. Then he sautés the onions, garlic and chilli in olive oil, adds salt, pepper and tomatoes, and serves our fresh medley of seafood, poached in a spicy tomato sauce, atop steamed rice.

"Divine," I pronounce as we eat, seated on the shore, sharing a bottle of wine and watching the sunset, "I had no idea you were such a good cook!"

DAY TWO
Kenepuru Sound to Picton

In the morning there's no sign of Bob in the cottage but when I look out over the bay I see him on the rocks, fishing line in hand. I make bacon and egg sandwiches and a thermos of tea and wander over with this picnic breakfast.

"You know," he says, after we've sat together quietly for a while admiring the scenery, "it's so peaceful here I could stay forever." He yanks the line and continues. "Whenever I'm stressed out and want the world to stop, I'm going to think of this moment, sitting here with a rod, and all the clean, green and fresh sights, sounds and smells of New Zealand," he says, suddenly laughing at himself and tossing me his camera. "Quick take a photo and bottle the moment, I'll use it as a screensaver!"

We enjoy our breakfast quietly on the rocks then, as the fish aren't biting, pack our gear and reluctantly catch our water taxi ride back to Te Mahia. When we get to the other side Bob consults his watch."I guess it's time to drive to Picton," he says sadly.

"I guess so," I reply, also feeling glum.

We drive back to Linkwater and reconnect with Queen Charlotte Drive, winding through several gorgeous bays and headlands offering fantastic views of the Queen Charlotte Sound. At the Picton lookout we stop to watch the Interislander Ferry pull into the terminal at the western end of Picton's palm-lined foreshore.

We find a quiet place to park and then Bob begins the enormous task of sorting out his collection of souvenirs. I give him a hand. Out comes the box of macadamia butter toffee crunch from Kerikeri, pumice from Lake Taupo, hand knitted jumpers from Geraldine, soaps from Thames, paua shells from the Catlins and so it goes on...

"Ugh!" I say, pulling out a crab's claw from Waipu that mysteriously made its way into the boot, "Do you really want to keep this?"

"Oh yes," says Bob vehemently, taking it and packing it away carefully.

"You're going to weigh a ton when you fly home," I warn, eyeing the enormous pile of bottles, bags and other paraphernalia stacked beside the car.

"Oh yes," says Bob, rubbing his belly like a satisfied Buddha with a cheeky grin and a glint to his eye, "especially after helping you to eat your way around New Zealand!" ■

Nelson to Picton:
Attractions and Activities

Creative Flair: Havelock
Greenshell Mussel Cruise: www.mtrav.co.nz
Kayaking: www.hopewell.co.nz
Compass Charters: compass-charters.co.nz
Water Taxi: arrowwatertaxis.co.nz
Pelorus Sound Water Taxi: Havelock
Queen Charlotte Track: www.qctrack.co.nz
Sea Kayaking: www.nzseakayaking.com
Affinty Cruises: www.affinitycruises.co.nz
Guided Walks: www.southernwilderness.com

Nelson to Picton:
Cafés and Eateries

Boat Shed Café: 350 Wakefield Quay, Nelson
Lambretta's Café Bar: 204 Hardy St, Nelson
Pelorus Bridge Café: RD2, Rai Valley
Mussel Boys: 73 Main Rd, Havelock
Fat Cat Café: SH6, Havelock
Dog & Frog Café: 22 High St, Picton
Barn Café: 48 High St, Picton

Portage, Marlborough Sounds - Deerace Publishing

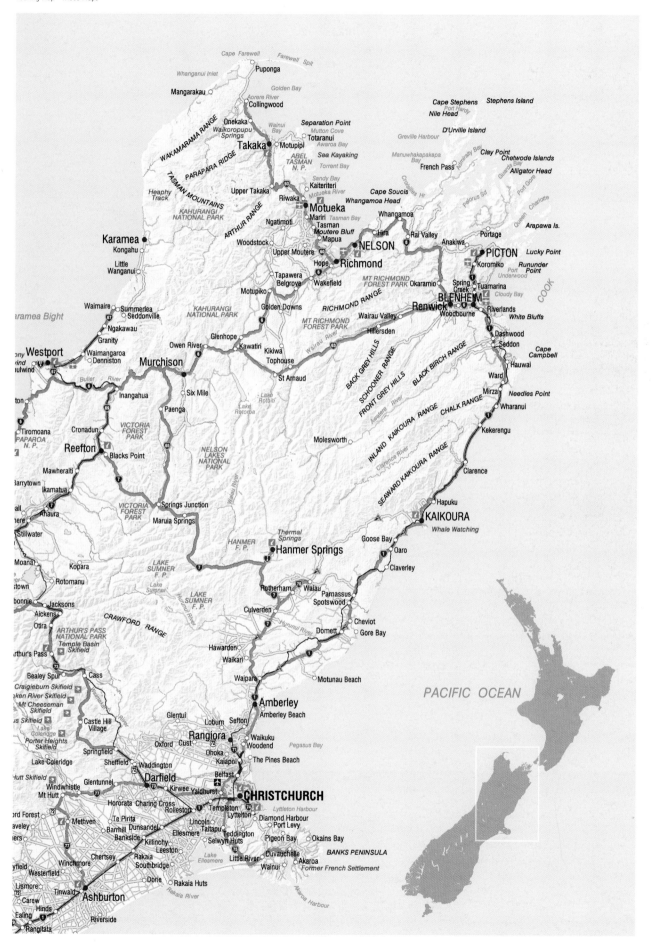

TAKE THE SCENIC ROUTE WITH APEX